NOT ON MY
WATCH

To Dane

My friend, brother, and seminary
comrade.
Thank you for all the memories
We share,

RCW
08/01/21

NOT ON MY
WATCH

*Practical Principles for Planting, Pastoring,
and Preaching the Word of God*

ROBERT L. WILLIAMS,
DMin

EQUIP PRESS

Colorado Springs

NOT ON MY
WATCH

Published by Equip Press, Colorado Springs, CO

"Unless otherwise noted, all Bible quotes in this text are attributed to the King James version."

First Edition: 2019
Not On My Watch / Robert L. Williams
Paperback ISBN: 978-1-946453-40-2
eBook ISBN: 978-1-946453-41-9

EQUIP PRESS

Colorado Springs

DEDICATION

Dedicated to my parents:
My dad for teaching me that working hard at noble things always pays off.
My mom for teaching me that looking into the face of Christ the Lord
is always the path forward.

I am doing a great work!
Why should it stop, while I come down to you?
—Nehemiah 6:3

CONTENTS

Dedication   5

Introduction   9

SECTION ONE
PASTORING ON HELL'S FRONT PORCH

1. The Cleansing of the Church   15
2. Spiritual Warfare and Church Growth   17
3. Gagging on Gnats While Swallowing Camels   21
4. Thugs in the Temple   25
5. Giving is the Biblical Method for Resourcing Ministry   29
6. Pastoral Pest Control   31
7. The Laborer Is Worthy of His Reward   35

SECTION TWO
PRACTICAL PRINCIPLES FOR PLANTING,
PASTORING, AND PREACHING

8. Proof That the Grace of God Had Changed My Life   41
9. Christ Is the Boss of Your Church and Your Calling   45
10. The Job of the Church Is to Grow the Word   51
11. The Church Is Commissioned to Produce Spiritual People   55
12. Old Testament Precepts for Leading New Testament Churches   59
13. Biblical Ignorance as Demonstrated By So-Called Evangelicals   65
14. Blessed Are the Dead Who Die in the Lord   69

15. God Speaks Clearly: Let the Property Go 75
16. The Call to Ministry Is Not Always a Call to the Pulpit 79
17. God Quickened When I Wanted to Quit 83

SECTION THREE
RACISTS ARE IN THE CHURCH
BUT NONE ARE IN CHRISTIANITY

18. Racism and Its Inception into the Human Race 91
19. Salvation Is the Antidote for the Poison of Babel 97
20. Speaking Against Racism from the Grave 101

SECTION FOUR
SEVEN EXPOSITORY SERMON OUTLINES

Jesus Is Our Hiding Place (Josh. 20:1–9; Ps. 32:7) 105
How to Stop the Plague (2 Sam. 24:17–25) 105
Instructions for Ministry (1 Sam. 8) 105
John the Baptist (Luke 1:18–20; 57–64; 67–80) 105
Required Reading from Ruth (Ruth 1:1-4:17) 106
Greater Heights of Kingdom Building (Hag. 1–2) 106
Faith and Prayer (Hab. 1–3) 106
Prayer from the Belly of Hell (Jonah 1:17; 2:1, 10) 106

INTRODUCTION

A BIBLICAL DEFINITION OF A NEW TESTAMENT CHURCH

Throughout the discussions in this book, the term "New Testament church" is repeatedly referenced. I offer this opening chapter as a definition of the purpose, structure, and characteristics of what a New Testament church is, in its essence.

God the Father established the church to be a spiritual community, which serves as a type of kingdom of heaven on earth. As such, the role of the church in the world is to exalt the risen Savior, educate the saved, and evangelize the world. The biblical method by which this is performed and how it is performed is rooted in a proper exegesis of Ephesians 4:11-12. Below are the verses in the King James translation and *Wuest's Expanded Translation of the New Testament.*

"And He gave some to be apostles, some to be prophets, some to be evangelists, and some to be pastor/teachers; for the perfecting of the saints, for the work of the ministry, for the edifying of the body of Christ" (Eph. 4:11-12).

"Jesus, he himself, no one else, gave or gifted men to be leaders of the church. He gave some to be 'apostles'" (Eph. 4:11a Wuest). This word speaks in context to the twelve apostles and in comparison, to all who proclaim the gospel. He gave some to be "prophets." This word refers not to foretellers of the future, but to expounders, explainers, and forth tellers of the gospel. He gave some to be "evangelists." This word speaks of those who are itinerant missionaries who carry the message of the gospel into foreign and homelands. He gave some to be "pastor/teachers." This word in Greek translates into two English words: pastor *and* teacher.

Thus, the person who leads God's people must possess the gift(s) of shepherding, which are leadership and teaching. These leaders are given to the church for the "perfecting of the saints." Worship is the activity within this spiritual community which exalts the glory of the name of Jesus Christ and promotes maturation. The "work of the ministry," the primary function of the New Testament church, is teaching and preaching, discipleship, the Word of God, and the education of the saints. The "edifying of the body," the ultimate result of our participation in this spiritual community, is reproduction, i.e., evangelism of the world.

God's people congregate in a spiritual community for the purposes of: exalting Christ which perfects the saints; educating the saved which is the work of ministry; and evangelizing the world which is building up the body of Christ by taking the glory of His name to the lost and dying world.

The administrative handbook of the New Testament church is the Pastoral Epistles. The structure of the New Testament church has three levels. The top represents the Head, who is the Lord Jesus himself. The second is the ordained level of elders. The third and final level of leadership is that of deacon/minister, which is where all believers fit. In addition, these books also give very clear instructions to church leaders and members about how we are to behave in the house of God.

Finally, Jesus prayed for the church in John 17. In these verses (13-26), he gives us a very clear picture of the church and His desired characteristics for it. My definition of a New Testament church can be summarized in the prayer that Jesus prayed for us in John 17. Therefore, the characteristics of a New Testament church are unity and oneness (v. 11); joy that is not tethered to the world (v. 13); distinction and separation from the world (v. 17); behaviors within and without the body that honor the Son (v. 21). Last, but certainly not least, Jesus asked the Father for us to display the love of God to the world and one another (v. 23). Jesus prays that we are capable of living as though we are experiencing the love of God on a daily basis and a personal level (v. 25). These characteristics must be ever-present in a body of believers if they are to be a New Testament church. Remove or replace any of them with anything, and you have lost the essence of a New Testament church as prayed for by the Son of God.

SECTION ONE

PASTORING ON
HELL'S FRONT PORCH

CHAPTER 1

THE CLEANSING OF THE CHURCH

My house shall be called the house of prayer,
but you have made it a den of thieves.

—Matthew 21:13

In a church 190 years old or 190 days old, it is not uncommon to find layer upon layer of tradition, history, and cultural activities which have absolutely nothing to do with being a New Testament church. This church was my first pastorate and it met only twice a month for worship. On the calendar for my first ninety days were eight fundraisers events, but only six worship events. The scheme was to use the two Sundays on which there was no worship as fundraisers for any auxiliary in the church, as well as other community organizations that had pseudo-religious connections to the church, such as the Burial Society. Yes, the Burial Society! They raised money for the maintenance of the cemetery, one that had not been cared for very well. Other abnormalities included a church with 120 members having six different choirs, each with its own paid musician. Also, every auxiliary in the church, about nine of them, had its own treasurer and bank account. If a choir had a fundraiser for their anniversary and raised a hundred dollars, they kept those funds to themselves, but the church paid the musician, purchased the robes, and paid the utilities, along with all other costs. The point is, the auxiliaries owned their funds, not the church.

On the day of my installation, one of the oldest deacons of the church came to me and said that he had been praying for years that God would send a young seminary-trained pastor to lead their church. I thought that was an indicator that they wanted to be brought into the twentieth century, as it relates to things like tithing, rather than raising money to fund the ministry and worshipping every Sunday, as well as conducting a midweek Bible study. These things were nothing big or earth-shattering, just the normal things that most churches had been doing for the last ten decades. I have never misread anyone as I did this dear deacon.

Seven months later, when I began to remove their nonbiblical practices, the same deacon shook his finger in my face and declared, "You are straight out of hell for destroying this church." I started with removing the pictures of all the former and dead pastors hanging on the back wall of the sanctuary. There arose no small stir about the desecration of the church's history and the honor and memory of those men. I cannot describe the darkness and the misery of preaching for six months while looking at the portraits of dead men. I moved those portraits to the farthest, most obscure corner in the building, and thought that was a compromise because my first inclination was to archive them in a storage box.

The principle taught through this experience is that there is but one gospel, and nothing or no person should interfere with the preaching and teaching of that gospel. Any person, place, or thing that does interfere should and must be dealt with to maintain the character of the church. Paul taught Timothy to instruct the believers that they avoid, remove, and disallow anything that subverts the preeminence of the gospel of Jesus Christ (Colossians 1:18). It does not matter how long the tradition has been accepted, nor does it matter how dear the congregation holds to it; if it subverts, it is wrong and must be dealt with if one's intentions are to give the church a New Testament focus.

CHAPTER 2

SPIRITUAL WARFARE
AND CHURCH GROWTH

*Now the Spirit speaks expressly, that in the latter times some shall
depart from the faith, giving heed to seducing spirits,
and doctrines of devils*

—1 Timothy 4:1

The greatest tool Satan has used against the church is biblical ignorance. The current American church model has been the model for more than fifty years. This model generally evaluates the size of facilities, finances, and fellowship as markers of whether or not a church is pleasing to God. However, none of these criteria are spiritual markers, but rather temporal and material. It has been my experience that there is little church growth without persecution. The Scripture bears this out in many instances. The church growth models of today experience little if any persecution. The plans do not even factor in such a thing as interference from the enemy. This growth model is mainly due to the mindset of "if you do things right" you will begin growing and continue to grow. Church growth as described in Scripture has as much subtraction as addition and an equal amount of multiplication (i.e., mission work).

My experience includes multiethnic churches, large and small Southern Baptist Convention churches, large and small traditional African American

Baptist churches, along with various church plants, both domestic and international. I have observed that fast and consistent church growth over an extended period is detrimental to the ability of a church to adopt a model of growth based on spiritual markers. Therein lie its weakness and its lack of relevance. Once the church plateaus, it goes into a state of preservation of its material self. It becomes a monument to God and has little or no spiritual impact on its community. That is as far from the New Testament church as one can be. It is exactly what the enemy has orchestrated to render the church spiritually ineffective. He has been extremely effective at this.

Some would eagerly argue this point, so I want to offer one example that is so disproportionately material and unspiritual that it is the only one needed to defend my point. Let us look at our facilities. Do you think God is pleased with us building multimillion-dollar sanctuaries that we use less than ten hours a week? Meanwhile, there are three billion people on the globe who live on less than USD 2.50 a day, and almost half of those live on less than USD 1.25 per day. According to UNICEF, 22,000 children die each day due to poverty. Yet, we build income tax-exempt organizations, which build tax-exempt properties with interest-bearing loans, and call that giving back to or blessing the community. Jesus Christ invested in people rather than property. Jesus Christ served people in the streets of their communities. He created the first-ever social safety nets for the poor, widows, orphans, and the infirmed.

We call ourselves evangelical when less than 1 percent of any Protestant church's membership has ever shared their faith with a non-believer, with a view of leading them to faith in Jesus Christ. The term "evangelical" in its etymology means to share the good news of Jesus Christ. It does not mean Republican, nor does it mean a strict biblical constructionist or conservative. Media networks and political pundits use this misapplication to describe a certain voter bloc. The misapplication of the word "evangelical" appeals to the biblically ignorant and leads them to believe that they are the moral and justice compasses of our nation. Even a casual study of Scripture will reveal that those who are evangelical do not support or vote for sexual harassers or those accused of sexual improprieties (national political context of late).

Paul said to Timothy, as it relates to growing the church at Ephesus: "For therefore we both labor and suffer reproach because we trust in the living God ..." Because the church, for the most part, walks by finances today, it has no experience in walking by faith. As a result, it is not in a position to please God. It is only by faith that God can be pleased.

CHAPTER 3

GAGGING ON GNATS WHILE SWALLOWING CAMELS

You blind guides, filtering out a gnat and gulping down a camel!
—Matthew 23:24 AMPC

"How to Be a Church Member and Go to Hell Anyway" was the title of a series I preached in my first pastorate. The point of this series was to focus on the things that church members consider sacred and accept as spiritual truth. Mainly, it demonstrated the fact that being religious and being rightly related to Christ are two very different things with very different destinies. The church was nearly 200 years old, and they held that fact high as proof that all they had done and were doing was satisfying and glorifying to God. The text of the series was Isaiah 1:1–3 and the points were Follow Your History (v. 1 with Isaiah 1:4), Follow Your Heart (v. 2 with Isaiah 29:12), and Follow Your Head (v. 3 with 2 Samuel 40:21).

During the invitation, after the last segment of the message, a 67-year-old grandmother came forward to accept Jesus as Savior and Lord. Her statement to me was, "Pastor, back when I was twelve years old, my mother made me sit on that bench right there until I joined the church. However, I have realized that, back then, I got religion, but today, I want to get

Jesus." At that moment, she could see the difference between religion and a relationship with Christ.

While this salvation delighted heaven and her pastor, it did not delight the members of the church. They attacked the woman as only church folk can do, verbally and by disassociating with her within their cliques. Some weeks later, I noticed that this sister was missing in worship and discipleship. I visited her in her home, and she shared with me the treatment she was receiving. They were shunning her and treating her as an outsider because, according to them, she had brought shame on the pastor who baptized her and all those who followed up to my tenure. These were people with whom she not only attended church but also had grown up and attended school. Nothing in my estimation illustrates "spiritual wickedness in high places (Eph. 6:12), the Church," as clearly as this incident.

One of the deacons approached me in the midst of the series and questioned my premise. He told me that the title of the series suggested that there are lost people in the church, and that I should preach more comforting messages. When I confirmed that there were lost people in the church and that he was exactly right concerning my premise, he went on to say, "Reverend (this particular deacon never referred to me as pastor over the course of twenty-two months), that's just not true. We have been a church for 190 years, and we have come this far by faith." This man and I never saw eye-to-eye on any spiritual issues. I contend the disagreements were due to the human (church) history, the human heart, and the human head, (I Cor. 2:14) because they are spiritually discerned.

When these things govern one's relationship—or lack thereof—with Christ, there is zero acknowledgment of the Word of God. Without such acknowledgment, it is impossible to know the will of God or to perform the work of God. The question the deacon asked me to argue his point was, "Reverend, how do you explain all these years of existence and these buildings and people who have faithfully lasted almost 200 years?" My reply was a story I heard from a professor years earlier. There was a delegation of Chinese Christians who were brought to the United States to observe the success and largess of the Baptist church. Upon the completion of the trip, the Baptist leader asked the Chinese visitors what their observations had taught them. They replied, "We have learned and are amazed by the fact that the American church can accomplish so much without God."

As Paul left Timothy in Ephesus, his instructions were to preach the Word of God in-season and out-of-season. That is the mandate for every man or woman called of God to deliver the Word of God to the world. To use an adage, "The church today is too earthly minded to be of any Heavenly good." I contend this deacon thought this way because the church had taught him to think that way.

Following one's head is to do what is right in your own eyes (see Deuteronomy 12:8; Judges 17:6, 21:25). Following one's unredeemed heart is allowing the desperately wicked heart of man to dictate the basis upon which one relates to God (see Jeremiah 13:10, 17:9, 18:12). Following one's history is to allow cultural and historical people, places, and events to be a part of worship that is supposed to be completely dedicated to the preeminence of Christ (see Exodus 20:1-6; Colossians 1:18)

NOT ON MY WATCH

CHAPTER 4

THUGS IN THE TEMPLE

And I will put a division and a sign of deliverance between My people and your people. By tomorrow shall this sign be in evidence.

—Exodus 8:23

On Thursday, after the mountaintop experience of the first Sunday, I received a phone call and found myself in the valley of despair. The dissenting leaders had disconnected the electrical power; therefore, we would not have access for Sunday. It was a hot Georgia August, and the windows were not designed to open; there was no ventilation or light. Having older members who could not handle that type of environment, we could not worship in the sanctuary. God encouraged me with these words spoken to Moses concerning the plague of flies: "And I will put a division between many people and thy people: tomorrow shall this sign be" (Exodus 8:23). There were certain people in that church that God had called me to rescue or deliver from the darkness that held a death grip on the church. God said, "I have a plan for rescuing my people, and I will point them out to you." His plan of rescuing the saved from among the perishing was revealed over the following years. However, it was now time to rescue the building from the lost.

Sometime before sunrise on Friday of that week, I woke up with these instructions: call the alarm company, power company, and a locksmith, setting simultaneous appointments. Using the tire iron from my truck, I removed the exterior door, and the alarm technician disconnected the alarm so it would not place calls, alerting the dissenters. The alarm technician also changed the codes, password, and call list. The locksmith changed all exterior locks and opened all safes, as well as removed more than a dozen interior locks on everything from the kitchen and refrigerator, to file cabinets and more. The power company restored power to the building. It took most of the day for all the work to be finished. I left about 3:00 p.m. to go home and grab some white paint and brushes because I had scratched the door while removing it with a tire iron. My kids were home from school, and my daughter wanted to ride with me to paint the door. As always, we had a great time talking and answering her questions about the dissension in the church and why I was doing this very hard thing. As I was closing up the paint and getting ready to leave, one of the dissenters drove up. Soon after, a police car arrived with sirens blaring and lights flashing.

The dissenter had called the authorities to report a break-in. The officer clearly had a friendly relationship with the dissenter. After being accused of breaking into the church, I explained to the officer that I had painted the door and was preparing to leave. The officer told me to sit in my vehicle and not to leave. In his attempt to resolve the situation, the officer spoke to the dissenter, then came over to the truck, explaining that the dissenter wanted me arrested for trespassing and attempted breaking and entering. I explained to the officer that the majority of the congregation had called me and the dissenter was dissatisfied. The officer decided he needed to call his supervisor because he did not know what to do.

While awaiting the arrival of the supervisor, the dissenter came over to my truck, fussing and cussing at me for everything imaginable, all in the presence of my daughter! My daughter was furious, and I had to calm her down several times as this man verbally attacked me. I, on the other hand, stayed cool and played the role of peacekeeper. When the supervisor arrived, he asked who had the keys to the building. The dissenter insisted he had them, and that was why I was trying to break in. I told my side of the story and indicated that this man did not have the key to the building. I explained that he had walked out on the congregation the previous Sunday, threatening them with lawsuits since he was no longer allowed to lead. This statement infuriated the dissenter, and he railed at me, repeatedly stating that he was the vice chairperson of the church deacons and held keys to the church. The police supervisor asked him to open the door. He tried, but his key did not open the new lock. His face went pale, and he began to scream at the top of his lungs, demanding my arrest. I explained that another church leader had the key and offered to call him to come open the door. The supervisor declined and told me I could leave.

All the way home, I thought through the events of the day and explained to my daughter why I did not fight back when the dissenter was attacking me. I knew that what God wanted to happen had taken place, and I did not need to be drawn into a war of words with a man on the wrong side of God. My sweet daughter and I often talk about this experience, and she reminds me that if I ever need someone to attack that person, she is still ready. To this day, when I need my spirit lifted, or my hope replenished, I look at these events and praise the Lord. This experience was my sign that what happened the previous Sunday was nothing short of a miracle. God was now completely and firmly on the way to the rescue of His people from the "church thugs" who had been holding them hostage as they attempted to serve the Lord Jesus Christ.

The next battle for the soul of this church took place in a judge's chamber over the next six months. The dissenters sued the church and me because, according to them, the vote was not conducted according to the bylaws. They were seeking a restraining order and a new vote. Three months into this personally humiliating trial, the judge ruled that there would be no restraining order, but he would require the church vote again. It took nearly two months for this to happen because of the bylaw requirements. When the vote was finally taken, all the people who walked out of the church on that first Sunday came back for the first and only time. The vote went according to plan, and the majority voted for me again. The judge took these results and concluded that the case was being dismissed with prejudice, and he informed the dissenters that if they wanted to be a part of this church, they had to work it out with me. They called the judge and me a few non-Sunday school names. After we left the courthouse, they were never heard from again.

The Lord taught me several things through this experience. First, He taught me that miracles require some manual labor on the part of the believer. Next, He showed me that the battle is the Lord's. We simply report for duty. Thirdly, He taught me to rejoice and to be exceedingly glad when men revile and persecute me for His namesake (Mt. 5:1). Fourthly, the sending of Christ to the cross shows us all how God will stop at nothing to deliver His people from the powers of darkness. Fifth, in every church, no matter how misguided it may be, God has a remnant, and if they pray for deliverance, they will receive it. Sixth, God showed me that there were some special people in that church who were dear to God, and He heard their prayers and sent a deliverer to free them from the bondage of those church thugs. Seventh, looking back upon these events years later, God demonstrated that He would use His enemy to procure the deliverance of His people. Many of those people who helped us through these tumultuous times were later revealed to be on the side of the enemy, and eventually, God pruned them from the body as well. However, they were instrumental in our getting through the first twelve months. Finally, more than anything else, I learned that Christianity is intensely spiritual, perfectly natural, and thoroughly practical.

CHAPTER 5

GIVING IS THE BIBLICAL METHOD FOR RESOURCING MINISTRY

I will freely sacrifice unto thee: I will praise thy name, O LORD;
for it is good.

—Psalm 54:6

One of the areas of discipleship that gets a disproportionate amount of pulpit time is, sadly, one of the least practiced in many churches; the principle of giving tithes and offerings to God. One of the challenges I faced in the process of aligning a church with the New Testament church structure was getting church members to give the tithe and offering. The institutionalized church, with its many shades of tradition, culture, and biblical ignorance levels, has created a membership who must be sold something — a dinner, a pie, a raffle ticket, or an admission fee — in order to finance the church. The art of giving and trusting God has vanished. The church of Christ, who is truly His bodily manifestation in the world today, must function simultaneously in the spheres of preaching and practice. The principles we preach must be wedded to practice because theology without practical application is worthless.

For instance, many Protestant churches use verses such as Malachi 3:8–10 and 2 Corinthians 9:7 as their basis for the giving of the tithe and offering to the Lord. While the church preaches and teaches this as frequently as they sing "Amazing Grace," they sell everything from fish dinners, potato pies, and chicken dinners to candy apples. The list continues with the taxations, fees, and dues for various special days, not to mention the different offerings taken in almost all auxiliaries. When the trait of raising money for ministry is substituted for the cheerful and willing tithe and offering, the giver is deprived of one of the most valuable and comforting graces we receive from God the Father, through God the Son, and by God the Holy Spirit at salvation, which is the joy of sowing and reaping. When we are motivated by the thing we get for the money, the biblical method of giving the tithe and offering is subjugated and circumvented, and all we get for it is the fish or chicken dinner. However, when we, by faith, give the tithe and offering, we get to see God bless and multiply our little bit and make much of it. We get to see our seed of faith grow for us, although we gave it away to Him. He then uses it to bless so many others.

When I initially introduced this idea my first pastorate, a traditional church, there was much disdain and disgust for the idea of taking away the church anniversary, pastor's anniversary, choir anniversary, and their fundraising capabilities. One of the women in the choir, a deaconess, stood and attacked me with mean-spirited words, yet with sweet southern charm. After trying several ways to get me to allow the choir to raise money, she had had enough of me. With one hand on her hip and the other pointing at me, she said, "Well, I've got news for you, you won't get enough money out of us to pay the light bill or your salary until you restore our right to raise money for our church." That was not the last I heard from her until she left the fellowship. Be that as it may, this 190-year-old church gave more in nine months through the practice of willfully and cheerfully giving the tithe and offering, than they had ever raised in an entire year. When God sets a principle in place, it is for our good not His. When the church allows God's biblical principles to be changed, it is always to the detriment of the church. The lesson here is no matter who or what comes against leadership that is within the biblical frame of reference, it cannot stand, and it will always lose.

CHAPTER 6

PASTORAL PEST CONTROL

This know also, that in the last days perilous times shall come,
lovers of pleasures more than lovers of God; having a form of
godliness, from such turn away.

—2 Timothy 3:1–5

Most pastors can relate to the syndrome, or might I say "sin-drome," of members nesting in ministry areas. This is when a few church members, led by one of their peers, takes up permanent residence in some ministry area and make it off-limits to others. I have experienced this in many areas. One in particular is the kitchen, but this can creep into any ministry of the church, including ministry boards, committees, and leadership. This is a form of a clique within a congregation. It is bred by the lack of knowledge of the church organizational structure as stated in the Pastoral Epistles. It is a form of power staking and a means and platform for protesting. No ministry area is off-limits.

Some pastors come into a church where this has been tolerated and permitted by those who came before them, while others have observed this develop under their leadership but refused to address it. The bottom line is

Sh. = Shunning. Apparently a common practice in AA Church communities.

that this is a platform for Satan, and just as in all nests, there can be filth. In a bird's nest or a rat's nest, one will find not only babies (undiscipled babes in Christ), but also all sorts of trash and uncleanliness. Mice for instance, perform all of their bodily functions in that nest. The nest is the place of their total existence until they are old enough to leave. Such is the case with church nesters. They handpick those who will be loyal to them over any other leaders in the church. They will often defer to the lead rat when deciding whether the pastor or other leadership is to be followed. Church nesters will often come to church but seldom and, in some cases, never attend Bible study or worship.

Everything centers on the nest leader and their instructions for those often biblically ignorant church members who think they are doing the right thing by following the leader of the nest, I discovered this to be the case in several of my pastorates and learned to tear up the nest and clean out the mess. The one I will discuss for this section was a kitchen ministry taken over by a woman who disliked the new pastor and was not going to allow him or his influence in her territory. This sister was old enough to be my grandmother. She had been in that church longer than I had been in the world. She was not cordial or loving to anyone except the other rats in the nest. She went out of her way to make it known that any of her folks who showed loyalty to the pastor would be out of her graces. She kept a loyal following with food. She spent the church's money to purchase meals for Wednesday night fellowship and special events, always buying extra, so her crew had plenty to take home afterward. The straw that broke the proverbial camel's back was a poorly prepared meal, by design, for some white missionaries who were visiting our fellowship.

That was when I knew I had to deal with the situation for the sake of the spiritual health of the church. We discuss racism in another chapter, but for now let it suffice to say that if a pastor tolerates any form of racism, he is willfully agreeing to side with the enemy of God and to disagree with God. The mindset of any church nester can be characterized as one of defiance—no one, including God, tells him or her what to do. Discipleship is off-limits, as is worship. This group huddled to themselves and purposely avoided the rest of the congregational activities. This particular lady made sure I saw her before or after church, but never in discipleship nor worship. As discussed in the opening chapter, the principle of "no discipleship means no leadership" was applied, and that included the kitchen. The half-dozen of them were confronted with their lack of attendance and notified they would be removed from the kitchen ministry unless they began to worship and study with the rest of us. We set a date and when it arrived, all of them, except for one lady, stopped coming altogether. In the kitchen, we found all kinds of mess and misappropriated church funds, as well as property for personal gain and bribing. Once the leadership principle was applied, we regained control of our meals, both quality and quantity, as well as the physical space of the kitchen itself. When asked about the kitchen ministry, the leader said, "I have been serving in this church for a long time, and this is how I serve God." Nonetheless, when confronted with reasonable requirements, she quit the church altogether. Rather than subject herself to genuine spiritual discipline and growth, she packed up her kitchen and went home.

CHAPTER 7

THE LABORER IS WORTHY
OF HIS REWARD

Or Delivered from cancer and debt!

Let the elders that rule well be counted worthy of double honor

—I Timothy 5:17

A friend and former seminary classmate has been pastoring the same church for over three decades. He has had some issues that defy logic and certainly biblical teachings about the care and compensation of church leaders. This story is added to encourage young church and ministry leaders not to be so focused on the needs of the congregation that you neglect your personal needs and those of your family.

After more than twenty years leading his congregation as a pastor/teacher, Tom was diagnosed with cancer. While he was telling me the diagnosis and the treatment process following surgery, he paused and said that was the least of his problems. I couldn't imagine anything more problematic than his disease and the arduous treatment plan, so I waited for him to complete his statement. He said, "The church does not provide me with any insurance, including health insurance. I will be indebted to the medical industry for the rest of my life should I survive the disease!" He went on to add, "I am truly more afraid of the debt than I am of the disease." I was shocked, heartbroken, and angered by those words.

Here was a man of God that had given all he had to a congregation. They were giving praise and pomp for God's great work through him but not providing him with the necessities of life. This happened before healthcare and its cost was a national debate and crisis. It was a crisis to this brother in the Lord, so I immediately began to search for solutions for his dilemma. The first place my mind went was the church. They were in a building fund campaign, so I said to Tom, "Your church needs to cover the cost of your medical care out of the building fund if those are the only funds they have to pull available. The church would do well to forget the building for now. Taking care of their pastor should be the first and corporate desire of their hearts." He began to explain to me that the church was ready to begin building, the loan was approved, the bids let, the contractor chosen, and the money for the building could not be touched for any purpose other than the building of a new sanctuary. We prayed and ended our phone call.

I continued to pray, especially for the debt. I knew that God could heal my friend's body and would do so in any way he chose to, but I prayed more for the hearts of the people in that church. These people were depending on this servant of God to bring them a word from the Lord, to lead them in the paths of righteousness, and to bury their dead, marry their children, and pray for their infants. I prayed that their hearts would be turned to the needs of Tom and that their love for him would be moved to action.

After many months of recovering from surgery, the effects of chemotherapy, and radiation therapy, Tom returned to the pulpit. He was presented that day with a check from the church, which came out of the building fund, to cover all of his medical bills. The deacon who presented the check said, "Had we been more thoughtful of you and your needs we would have had insurance in place for you. But we have the deep conviction from the Lord Jesus Christ that you are more important to our future and us than a new sanctuary, so we are giving you this because of the depth of our love for our pastor/teacher."

Tom called that Sunday evening to tell me of this miraculous occurrence. He jokingly asked if I had put a bug in the ear of his deacons because they had done exactly what I suggested they do several months back. As we both wept for joy, I told him that I merely put the bug in the ear of the One who sits at the right hand of God, continually making intercessions for us (Heb. 7:25). Praise His name, He did the rest. The church subsequently purchased health insurance for Tom and his family.

SECTION TWO

PRACTICAL PRINCIPLES
FOR PLANTING, PASTORING,
AND PREACHING

CHAPTER 8

PROOF THAT THE GRACE OF GOD HAD CHANGED MY LIFE

Overcoming anger,

*Who shall change our vile body ... He is able even to subdue
all things unto Himself.*

—Philippians 3:21

As a child and young adult, an uncontrolled temper was one of my greatest character flaws. I was born a brawler. I was ready to fight at a moment's notice and anger had a definite and certain control over my life. I'd rather fight than argue. It is still a part of me, but the Holy Spirit controls it. Early one Sunday morning, I was in my study getting ready for my discipleship class when the elder of finance came in to talk about finances and the checkbook. I was perturbed by this, as I have always taught that Sunday was for worship and nothing else. When I refused to discuss this with him, he became irate and insisted I stop putting him off. Again, I insisted that we could have this discussion any day but Sunday. As I gathered my notes and stepped out from behind the desk, the elder stood blocking my passage with his body and placed both his hands on my chest to stop me. When his hands touched me, I was immediately inflamed with anger and went into fight mode. I did not fight, however. Instead, I saw his irritation and tried to calm him by explaining my desire and practice to not do secular work, even for the church, on Sundays.

By the grace of God, I was able to teach my class, preach, and lead worship without anyone knowing what had occurred. Afterward, I sent the kids home with their mother, and when the building cleared, I went to my office and cried like a baby for some time. I was crying out of sheer anger. My body was trembling, and I was completely overcome by the incident. Then I cried more because I saw the hand of the enemy, attempting to gain a stronghold in our new and spiritually growing fellowship. I continued to cry because this gentleman had not heard a word I had been saying about the sanctity of the Lord's Day, and he obviously did not care about helping me focus on the teaching of the Word of God that day. Something as insignificant as balancing a checkbook was used to attempt to deflect us from worshipping the LORD in the beauty of holiness (Psalm 29:2) and from spirit and truth worship (John 4:24). I cried still more as I acknowledged the plume of anger welling up inside of me because I did not hit back. I am crying as I relive these moments that I consider some of the most emotionally painful in more than thirty years of ministry.

Within two weeks, this man and his family left the church, and it was twelve years before I heard from him again. I received a phone call from him requesting a meeting. I put it off a couple of times, mainly because I suspected my old temper still wanted me to take the swing at him I felt he was due. Finally, I agreed to meet with him at a Huddle House one morning. At that time, he immediately apologized for the incident. He confessed to having made other spiritual mistakes because what he had been taught and shown to be the church was so different from the view I was trying to instill of the church of Jesus Christ. He went on to say that over the years since we parted, he had come to understand the difference between the two views. He said, "Your view can be proven by Scripture and the other cannot. I want to worship God according to Scripture, and I want to grow spiritually. If you accept me, I want to join your church."

Since that day, we have had more time together than before the incident, and those times have been some of the best of our church family. As for the swing I wanted to take for more than a decade, I no longer wanted to take it after that meeting. This man has done what many a church member needs to do—walk away from that which does not look, act, feel, or practice the Word of God.

God, in His foreknowledge, saw that I needed a soldier at my side to hold up my arms, lift my spirit, and counsel my heart and mind as a brother in the Lord. God understood the need in my life and ministry and provided for my needs through the restoring of this relationship. The reconciliation with this man was the foundation for God providing counsel and companionship. Over the years, we have met somewhere for breakfast or lunch at least twice a month. Other men have joined us. Humility is a key trait in a pastor and teacher. This experience did so much for and to me, and I pray it has for my dear brother as well. We have seen God use relationships like these as the spiritual support system of our church. Only the blood of Jesus Christ can accomplish that in the hearts of men.

CHAPTER 9

CHRIST IS THE BOSS OF YOUR CHURCH AND YOUR CALLING

And he is the head of the body, the church: who is the beginning, the firstborn from the dead; that in all things he might have the preeminence.

—Colossians 1:18

There is nothing on the earth as strong, as big, and as powerful as the Word of God. The only thing that comes close is the craftiness Satan himself. Therefore, the growth of the Word of God within the church and the individual believer is of utmost importance and crucial to the spiritual well-being of both. The stories in this book are penned to encourage pastors to preach the Word of God in-season and out-of-season and for the believer to grow in grace through the study of the Word of God.

Dr. Harwood Steele, a professor of mine in Bible college, had impressed me with this saying: "Boys, when God places you in a new pastorate, and you go in and try to change everything you don't like all at once, the only thing you end up changing is the name of the pastor." Truer words have seldom been spoken. In my earliest pastorate, I was the youngest and the first seminary-educated pastor this church had ever called. I spent a great deal of time trying to reach the new congregation. I did very little besides pulpit preaching during the first six months. My goal was to evaluate and monitor the church at work and pray through the upcoming changes. During those months, we had several deacons' meetings, and I was beginning to feel as though I was getting to know the church and its leaders.

At the seventh deacons' meeting, we were to discuss and vote on the changes I would be imposing. At that meeting, I was introduced to five deacons who were attending their first church event in over six months. I was thoroughly taken aback by the fact that these near strangers could come in and monopolize the meeting as they did. Not only had they been absent from deacons' meetings, but also worship, discipleship, and fellowship.

As a young pastor, I began to explore ways to deal with this unspiritual habit of leaders. As I thought back to my childhood days of church, I recalled that there were several men in my home church that operated with this reckless attitude of seniority as the only qualification for serving God. I set aside everything to address this issue. I saw this as far more important than the other things I had planned. The question was how to do it. For any pastor dealing with this same issue, the answer is to teach and apply the leadership principles of the pastorals, choose and change leaders to get biblically qualified persons into leadership roles, and to pray for the providential hand of God to move those who fight the requirements that the head of the church Himself has set.

Upon examining the biblical qualifications for deacons and studying the usage of the term within and without the Scriptures, I discovered several problematic issues within the structure of this church, as well as many churches across the country. In the Pastoral Epistles (1 Timothy, 2 Timothy, and Titus), there are elders and deacons mentioned as church leaders. Both of these offices come with biblical requirements, detailing the moral and spiritual fitness required to serve in those capacities. The first issue I had was with deacons serving in the capacity of elders. The second issue arose from the presence of biblically unfit men attempting to lead a spiritual organization, without the mantle of anointing. The third issue was that there was another group of men serving as trustees (not corporate officers). The office of trustee is not mentioned as a church office in scripture; therefore, these men had met no biblical requirements to lead. The fourth issue was the congregation's inability to discern the difference. The principle I learned from this, and use to this day, is that if you don't have time for discipleship, we don't have time for your leadership. This rule, when applied, drains the swamp and exposes those who are there for themselves versus those who are there for the glory of Christ.

I spent twenty-two months engaged in the above and saw God do some of the most amazing things in that congregation. All of the leaders in question either resigned, got sick and were replaced or were buried. At one meeting held in my absence, one of the men used the entire meeting to rant about me and my foolish requirement that leaders attend Bible study. There was a virtual lynch mob organized, and my job was hanging in the balance. We met monthly, and on the day of our next meeting, I was prepared for a fight. Before I arrived at the church that Tuesday evening, I received a phone call from the same man's wife asking me to come to the hospital to pray with him, as he was very ill. I went, I prayed for and with them both, and left to return to the meeting.

The meeting concluded, and before I could get home, I was called again. The man had taken a turn for the worse, and when I arrived the second time, he was constrained by four leather straps on his hands and feet. The sheets were bloody from the abrasions where the constraints held him. The man was dead and, apparently, had fought his way into eternity. His wife was in shock, traumatized by what had occurred, and, surprisingly, was nicer to me than ever before. Her words were, "Pastor, he was so angry. Deep down in his soul, he was angry at you." I was the focus of his anger, for sure, but he was angry with God because of his preconceived notion of who could lead a church and how that church should function. The scriptures and the spirit of God had challenged his expectations. The lesson here is that God will always clear the way for His Word to get to the lost.

I also recall the case of a woman who was the wife, mother, and sister of three of the unfit deacons. This lady was the church boss, and her son was her general. Her husband was pushed about with every strong wind.

47

The church finances and reports were being improperly handled, and when I made recommendations to rectify the issue, this lady took it upon herself to see me removed as pastor. At this time, I didn't know she was behind the tricks and traps that were set for me. I had requested a part-time secretary to help with organizing a church that had never had adequate record-keeping or publications. This lady's son insisted on hiring the person and hired a young lady with no secretarial skills who was considered a promiscuous lady. Within a few days, she began to act inappropriately with me and came to work scantily clad. I worked with her less than two weeks before dismissing her.

The son of the woman who was the church boss also counted the offering. He was the one who received the bank statements, signed the checks, and made all the deposits alone. He once went eight months without presenting a financial report. When I pressed the point, a financial report was finally presented to the congregation nine months after my tenure began. Once we resolved the location of records and put checks and balances into the accounting procedures, this entire family was antagonistic toward my leadership. The lady got sick and went into the hospital, and when I visited her over a period of months, she never said a word but chose rather to stare me down the entire time I was in the room. She never returned to church until the day of her funeral.

On that day, as the family walked in, one of the family members went into a convulsive fit, stiffened like a board, and began to gag as though choking on her tongue. The scene and the sounds were unnerving, to say the least. As soon as the family was seated in the church, the sky went from beautiful blue to dark blue and within minutes we were in a tremendous thunder storm. The rains came, the winds blew, and the thunder and lightning were loud and continuous. The storm was so severe as we started up the hill from the church to the graveyard, the undertaker called the pallbearers to remove the casket from the car and walk it up the rest of the way. Standing over that hole in the ground, I did the committal quickly. As soon as we started down the hill, the storm subsided, the sun came out, and there was a rainbow in the sky.

To be clear, I am not intimating in any way that the above incidents were caused by anything to do with me or that they were the results of the opposition the people posted against me. The principles to learn here are numerous. Christ is the one who called you to ministry and to the church. You are leading; therefore, you do not need to know who or where the opposition is coming from. Don't waste time looking for it. Christ will not abdicate control of your call, tenure, or effectiveness to the people he placed you there to lead. Preach and teach the Word of God, and God will fight the battle and reveal the opposition when and if He desires.

CHAPTER 10

THE JOB OF THE CHURCH IS TO GROW THE WORD

But the word of God grew and multiplied.

—Acts 12:24

The craftiness of the god of this world has co-opted the mission of the New Testament churches, and the people are unaware. Case in point, the church I grew up in was a staunch Baptist church in the south. We were not very well-discipled in scripture but we knew God loved us, Jesus died for us, and why we were Baptist. Today that church is full bore Pentecostal, apostolic, and holiness, and the people are not aware of the fundamental doctrinal changes which have occurred. They are going along because the pastor said so; therefore, it must be right. In 2002, I began ministry in a new church. I was reluctant but commandeered by the will and spirit of God to assume this charge. I promised God that I would follow the biblical dictates to structure and build this body of people into a New Testament church. My exact words that day in my study were, "Lord if I must go, allow this work to be an experiment in the lab of the world for building and maintaining a New Testament church." I can say after fifteen years of this experiment that God's results are far different from my expectations. These results have been nonetheless pleasing, powerful, and practical for

Q: Olford on preaching

& Threaten w/arrest

helping people grow spiritually. This discipleship-focused church growth model affects the new believer, the growing believer, and the going believer.

As I began this work, my experience included pastoring churches of singular and multiple cultures, pastoring large and small churches, planting a church, and training men to plant churches, both locally and internationally. Combined with my rigorous Bible training, I was prepared to lead. In a lecture series given annually at my seminary, Dr. Stephen Olford once said to us: "When God sends you to a church, forgetting all else, you must preach the Word of God until everyone there who is not inclined to the Word of God leaves. Then you must continue to preach the Word of God, in-season and out-of-season until God fills the church with those who are inclined to the Word. Then you can be the powerful body of Christ."

Q?

My experience and education, along with the above mandate from a choice mouthpiece of God Almighty, created crises the very first day. There was a group in the church who opposed the vote of the majority and immediately became adversarial. The deacon chairman called me the night of the vote and said, "I represent the leadership of the church, and I am advising you that, although you have been notified otherwise, we opposed the vote and you are not the pastor of this church. And if you appear on the Sunday you have chosen to start, you will be considered a trespasser, and we will swear a warrant for your arrest with the sheriff."

This group was opposed to me based on my interview with them and the search committee, as well as the preaching and teaching I had done in view of the call. Prayers from my prayer partners, family, and friends went up as I contemplated doing what God had called and equipped me to do versus taking the easy way out and deciding I had a reputation, a ministry, and a name to keep clean. God's response to our prayers was GO!

As I arrived for worship that day in August, I was determined to accomplish the will of God. I didn't go with a show of authority; rather, I went under the authority of Christ with meekness and humility. Promptly at 11:00 a.m., the deacons and trustees lined up across the front of the church, and the chairman read aloud the letter they had sent me reiterating

52

the phone conversation. After completing it, he looked at me and said, "Sir, you are trespassing." With that, the men lining the altar beckoned to their spouses, children, and others who followed them to stand up, and they all left the building immediately. As I recall, there were about 110 people in the church that day, and the crowd that left was at least forty people, representing no less than 70 percent of the income of the church. My thoughts went immediately to being arrested and going to jail, with my name and ministry scandalized in the papers. My throat went dry, my heart began to pound, and my hands began to sweat as I clenched my Bible and the spirit of the Lord said to me, "Never mind them; I sent you here to preach my Word."

When that crowd exited the building, it was as though thick and looming darkness was dispelled and replaced by the light of the world. My extemporaneous title and text were "There Is a Light: John 8:12." We had church as though none of the controversy existed, and the spirit of the Lord was outpoured and overflowing. Immediately following the benediction, the congregation called a business meeting to order and heard a motion to remove all the current deacons and trustees from office, on the grounds that they were spiritually unfit for leadership. (It is important to note that the individuals were removed from office, not from the congregation.) The motion was seconded and approved unanimously by those in attendance. This was an extraordinary move on the part of the Holy Spirit and a testimony to the power of God. I suspect this has not happened a dozen times in the entire history of the Baptist church.

The next six months were brutal and embarrassing as this group filed injunctions against the church and kept a smear campaign going within and without the church. However, the Word of God began to grow in the hearts and minds of the people who wanted to live and lead biblical, spiritual lives. On this first day of growth, God unusually grew the congregation from 160 people to less than 100. Over the years, the lesson learned is this: in biblical church growth, subtraction is as important as addition. Our society tells us that adding is the only way to grow a church, but the truth is, God has to move some things and people to aid the spiritual growth of the core.

Fifteen years after this initial day, God has steadily grown His word and this church. At 65 members today, this congregation is stronger and more spiritually engaging the world with the word of God. Financial giving is up per capita, missions giving and participation is up, and the church has served in local and international mission efforts that never existed or were even on the radar before the growth of the Word of God in the hearts of our people. One last fact about this: while the church was at 160, the average Sunday school attendance and mid-week discipleship was around 10 percent. Today, the average attendance for discipleship is closer to 50 percent. For a Southern Baptist church, that is an astounding fact that many of my colleagues would relish seeing on any given week of the year. The growth of the Word of God is the job of the church, not buildings, budgets, bus ministries, or other traditional programs and initiatives churches use. The focus of the New Testament church should be growing the Word of God alone.

As with the church in Acts 12, we too, went through persecution; however, with the prayers of the saints and the process of growth through the Word of God (discipleship), we are a spiritually stronger congregation.

CHAPTER 11

THE CHURCH IS COMMISSIONED TO PRODUCE SPIRITUAL PEOPLE

⸰ Labor not for the meat which perishes,
but for that meat which endures to everlasting life

—John 6:27

This chapter in the gospel of the beloved disciple opens with the miracle of the feeding of the five thousand. This miracle is the set-up for the remainder of the chapter and the foundation for our thesis in this lesson. It is a picture of the church, perhaps the first church, as Jesus was the shepherd and the disciples were the members. Those in the crowd were merely spectators. It was a large crowd, and they were following Him because they had seen the miracles Jesus had performed on the diseased.

Even today, the crowds that show up at our churches are, for the most part, spectators and miracle-seekers. They are not looking for the spiritual growth that comes from the Word of God and the inspiration of the Holy Spirit. At the feeding of the five thousand, there were twelve in the crowd with this desire; the rest were spectators. After years of pastoral ministry, I believe that fast (numerical) church growth is nearly always detrimental to the spiritual growth of the individuals in the church. First and foremost, the New Testament church should produce spiritual men and women or disciples of Christ. There is a reason why Jesus spent three years with twelve men as He set up the New Testament church. The reason is relational discipleship, which cannot be accomplished in large groups as effectively as in smaller ones.

As this chapter continues, Jesus is moved with compassion for the crowd. In addition, He seeks a means to feed them since the Passover was approaching. Meeting practical needs is the method Jesus most often used to introduce others to His message. The act of meeting practical needs has become a lost art in the church. Most Christians today feel they are doing mission work and serving the kingdom of God by solely giving a mission offering and going to the church campus for worship. The extent of most church members' involvement in missions is financial support. However, Jesus set an example in all the gospels of rolling up His sleeves and getting involved in lives to share the good news. Practical ministry and local missions are the missing elements of the New Testament church. Jesus asked Philip, "Whence shall we buy bread that these may eat" (John 6:5b)? The Holy Spirit adds via John, "This he said to prove him: for he knew what he would do" (John 6:6). Philip's response is typical of the church today: Throw money at the problem and feel good about your accomplishments for the kingdom, solving spiritual issues through finances rather than faith. How shall we serve these people? How can we help these people? How can we minister to these people? How can we be the church to these people? These are the questions that Jesus was asking.

The question in Verse 5 is answered in Verse 27. If the church is not producing spiritual results, it is not fulfilling the mission of the New Testament church. Jesus wanted to see if His teachings and examples were taking hold in the minds and hearts of His disciples. Philip proved they weren't. To him, the ministry was about money accomplishing that which the Son of God was requesting. So, in verse 26, Jesus says "The supernatural power of my Father who I've come to make visible and available to you is not why you are seeking me, but because you did eat of the loaves and were filled." In other words, the crowd was seeking Jesus for the same reasons large crowds show up in many sanctuaries today. They are looking to be entertained and satisfied socially or religiously, but not necessarily to become more spiritual. In the next verse, Jesus says that the church (the body of Christ, the people who are washed in the blood of Christ) is to labor not for the meat, food, church programs, and events which are earthbound and temporary. Things like buildings, budgets, and crowd sizes are the things the world uses to determine whether a church is successful. Jesus says here that a successful church is one that produces spiritual results in the lives of people. Buildings are not spiritual. They can be used for spiritual purposes, but they are not, in any way, spiritual. The church should be working for spiritual results, which the world does not measure and cannot see.

CHAPTER 12

OLD TESTAMENT PRECEPTS FOR LEADING NEW TESTAMENT CHURCHES

If you will walk in my ways, and if you will keep my charge, then
you shall also judge my house, and shall also keep my court

—Zechariah 3:7

~~◇ Pulpit furniture Light~~

One of the many traditions of the church has been the pulpit furniture and the place of the preacher during worship. It always seemed thrasonical to me for the preacher to be elevated in any way except for when he is preaching the Word of God. Over the years I grew tired of sitting on the pulpit in those big fancy chairs reserved for the preacher alone. At six feet tall and two hundred pounds, the chairs in this church dwarfed my stature. I could swing my feet without touching the floor if I sat back in it. Despite its soft cushions, the chair was an uncomfortable place for me to sit.

The location of the baptismal pool required us to move the furniture. Purely out of practicality, after baptism, I was led to leave the furniture out of the pulpit. I instructed the men not to return the furniture, and I would sit with the congregation in the pews. After worship, one of the sisters wanted to know why I did not put the furniture back in the pulpit. When I told her it would not be going back, and I would be sitting in the pews from now on, she blew a fuse and insisted we have a meeting, which I granted for the next afternoon.

At the meeting, this sister explained how disrespectful it was for me to remove the pulpit furniture. She went on to say she took food out of her children's mouths to help purchase that furniture. She insisted it was sacrilegious and that God could not be pleased with how I was defiling the sanctuary. She closed, saying that if the furnishings were not put back by the next Sunday, I would find myself in the fight of my life. I told her it was not going back because I did not like being on display, it was too large for the small area, and I wanted to worship sitting in the pew. The fight of my life never occurred; she decided to leave the church. When she left that meeting, she never came back. She attempted to poison the minds of others to do the same, to no avail!

There are several points in the confrontation that are worthy of expounding upon. First, there is the preeminence of Christ, not the pastor. The idea that the pastor is the highest figure in the membership is a lie straight out of hell. It lays a foundation for pride and vainglory. Jesus never distanced Himself from His disciples except to pray. He never put Himself up on a pedestal, except to allow large crowds to hear His words. There is an evil pride built into congregations' tradition and psyche, which has ruined many well-intentioned pastors. Pride is one of the easiest ways the enemy of God handicaps the church. Satan will allow us to be proud of our buildings, our crowds, our cash flow, and our celebration of ourselves to keep us from showing the world the glory of the Lord Jesus Christ.

Next, this confrontation points out how the practice of raising money to finance ministry creates an ownership mentality in the membership. This, of course, is also linked to pride but goes even further because it introduces the idea that the church and all its belongings are the property of the ones who raised the money. This begs for recognition of man over Messiah in the very place we supposedly have dedicated to the Lord Jesus Christ. This lady felt that this furniture belonged to her, and that she alone should determine how, when, and where it should be used, with no exceptions. That is the prevailing mindset of those who raise money for the resources of ministry. When one tithes and gives the Lord Jesus Christ the offering, he or she is doing just that, giving it to the Lord. Once we give it to Him, it is His; we no longer have any control of how He uses it for his glory. The acceptance of this spiritual principle of giving, this hand-off to God for His glory, is realized only by the giver. The raiser never transfers the goods to God; they remain in their possession because they did not give.

One more point needs to be made about this confrontation, and that is the trend of recognition of human material sacrifice in the Holy of Holies. Why is it that if you enter any sanctuary of any Protestant denomination, you will find the names of past and present members on the pews, the windows, the doors, the furnishings, and just about any other thing to which a brass nameplate can be attached? Because the tradition of the church, as unscriptural as it is, has led us to think that you and or your family are special because your names are on display in the church. That, in my opinion, is pimping out the church. The Bible clearly teaches us that what we do for and give to the Lord will be rewarded in heaven. No amount of earthly recognition is equal to heavenly rewards. The Bible also clearly teaches us that if we give or perform ministry tasks for earthly reward, that will be the only reward we will receive. The lady in this confrontation, according to her own words, put the satisfaction of the leadership of the church and her own desire to be recognized over the feeding of her children. The Bible never asks us to do ungodly things for the glory of God or the growth of the church. Satan alone is the propagator of such practices, and these practices are prevalent in the modern-day church.

One of the eight visions that Zechariah had is that of a restored Israel (3:1–10). These verses so aptly capture the essence of spiritual precepts and New Testament church leadership, grasping and acting on them by applying them to every situation of leadership. The pastor who desires a New Testament church where miracles take place must face the reality of venturing into enemy territory. The person of Satan is in your face and prepared to do hand-to-hand combat with you to prevent the turning of any church towards spiritual achievements. He will stop at nothing to prevent

①A prayer when faced by satanic opposition.
②A prayer for dis couragement, weariness, burnout.

NOT ON MY WATCH

Jesus Christ from robbing the grave again and taking back what the enemy has stolen. The reality is that the presence of Satan, as well as the presence of sin, stands in your path. He never takes holidays, vacations, or sick days. His work week is seven days and his workday is twenty-four hours with no breaks. Joshua was called to do a great work for the Lord, namely aiding in the restoration of Israel, but Satan was there to resist him in the person and power of sin.

Verse 2 teaches us that the leader of a New Testament church must have a rebuke for the enemy and that rebuke must have teeth. The Lord said to Satan, "The Lord rebuke thee." Just because Satan shows up does not mean his act will mess up the work of God. The halting and muting of his affect take place only when he is properly and appropriately rebuked. Over the years, I have developed a warfare prayer that I apply to any person, place, or thing that stands in opposition to the direction the spirit of God wants to lead His church. "Father, in the name of Jesus Christ, your son and my savior, and by the power of His blood, I rebuke..." The blank is filled in with the issue. I have prayed this prayer for many years, and I accredit its sufficiency with the push back my ministry has been able to apply to Satan himself. This verse inspired in me a battle mode that helped me get through some of the toughest spiritual warfare battles. It was victory in these battles that led to the taking back of churches that Satan had stolen and blinded. It gave me a Satan radar, which enabled me to spiritually sense the presence of evil and darkness. This was the prayer I used to rebuke Satan.

But there must also be a warfare prayer for the leader that rebukes depression, rejection, burnout, and just plain old weariness in the work of ministry. That prayer for personal warfare was, "Father in the name of Jesus, your son, and my savior, wash me in your blood, teach me your word, fill me with your Spirit, and use me for your glory." These prayers were and are my crutches, my invisible spiritual force field, which protected me and detected for me the attempts of the world, the flesh, and Satan himself to abort the work of the Lord. To summarize the importance of this type of rebuke, I borrow a line from an old American Express commercial: "Don't leave home without it."

Because of the reality of Satan's person, the presence of sin, and the need for rebuke power, there also has to be the imputation of righteousness into the body of Christ. Nothing does this but the preaching, teaching, fearing, and living of the Word of God. Nothing generates righteousness in the house of God but the Word of God. In verses 3–5, Joshua, the leader of Israel, appears in filthy garments. This is a picture of the righteousness of man and his attempts to please God without obeying God. One cannot obey God without understanding the Word of God and shedding the filthy rags of denominationalism, culturalism, traditionalism, and local churchianity.

It is reasonable to assume that if God has called you to lead a New Testament church, you will have to remove and dismantle some programs and practices of the local church that some will take as an affront to the very deity of Christ Himself. As with Joshua's clothing, they must be removed and replaced with alternatives given and sanctioned by the Word of God. Nowhere in Scripture are we instructed to celebrate the pastor's anniversary, the church's anniversary, or the choir's anniversary. These events are forced onto the calendar and routine activity lists. Filthy rags can be defined as anything God did not request or require. These things must come off as old dirty clothes if one expects to restore the broken church of the twenty-first century.

The church does not need to be restored because she has been doing the right things. The church cannot be restored with the programs and practices that tarnished her. Just as Paul uses the putting off of the old man and the putting on of Christ as an analogy for the individual believer, it must also apply to the church, and she indeed is in need of a change of garments. The robe and the fair miter are representative of a complete change of position and posture—an elevation. The things of the church, which God wants and decrees for His church, are superior to any program or experience that man, with all his power and money, can ever match. Joshua was being prepared for a higher work; a work higher than buildings, budgets, buses, and religious busyness. Joshua, was being prepared for the work of leading believers to spiritual maturity and utility in the kingdom of God. The Word of God is the garment and crown of his church.

In Verses 6–7, the angel of the Lord declares to Joshua the two requirements he must fulfill to achieve the will of the Lord as it relates to those people and their genuine and sincere desire to follow him. The angel of the Lord says to Joshua, "Walk in my ways." His ways are detailed in the words of the Bible, not in the history of a church. The second requirement is similar: Obey His instructions. These requirements refer to the precepts and the practice of the Word of God. It says nothing about pleasing a certain family or families, following a calendar or Sunday school quarterly, or adhering to dictates, be they mandates or suggestions.

Nothing in this verse indicates to a new pastor that he has to follow the program and the powers-that-be to keep his job. In fact, the latter part of this verse tells us that there are rewards for fulfilling the requirements. The rewards are greater than merely keeping our jobs. It says we will walk among the angels that stand near to the Lord Jesus Christ. To walk where these angels stand is to have eternal light in the darkest of times. It means to have eternal life in times of death. It means to have power and a hope that will never fade. It means to have the wherewithal to fight the good fight of faith.

Why must we fight for the relevance of the New Testament church? Because the church is not complete, and Satan is not yet confined. Moreover, because the believer must not be led to believe that a seat in the sanctuary takes the place of the hands, feet, heart, eyes, and voice of Jesus Christ in the streets.

CHAPTER 13

BIBLICAL IGNORANCE AS DEMONSTRATED BY SO-CALLED EVANGELICALS

Study to show yourself approved to God, a workman that needs not to be ashamed, rightly dividing the word of truth.

—2 Timothy 2:15

Prophetically, the Laodicean church represents the last era of church history and ushers in the rapture of the church. The Scriptures describe the Laodicean church as fat, rich, and complacent to the things of God. Their spiritual eyes were blinded by what they had, what they knew, and their worldly success. This church is disgusting to God, so He spews it out of His mouth. An introverted church is the state of the church before the rapture. In the last two presidential elections, the meaning of the word "evangelical," once defined as the biblically conservative movement, has been kidnapped and redefined by politicians and political pundits. In Christian theology, evangelism is the sharing of one's faith in Jesus Christ. Today it is misused to refer to those who vote conservatively along fiscal and social lines. This common misuse of the word robs it of its root meaning, which is to carry the gospel of Jesus Christ locally and internationally. The political pundits have hijacked the term, using it to identify a voting bloc, and churchgoers flock to it as though it makes them spiritual and right in God's eyes. However, they unwittingly fall for the ploy of our nation's political leaders to attract a certain voter demographic to certain political views.

The following statement is not a judgment of our country's most prolific evangelist, nor am I inferring he was not an evangelical. I am using this life experience to make a point for this chapter.

In 1982 or 1983, I attended a Billy Graham crusade in the Tangerine Bowl in Central Florida. By night, we were the counselors for the people giving their lives to Christ because of Dr. Graham's preaching. By day, we attended an assortment of courses on evangelism, as well as canvassed neighborhoods to share our faith and invite people to the crusade. One of the courses was on world religions. I sat and listened as the leaders called the Mormon religion a cult. It was further defined as such in several publications distributed to us by this ministry. In 2012, during the election for president, Dr. Graham chose to endorse a Republican Mormon over a Christian Liberal. What a difference twenty-nine years made in the way Christians viewed their impact on the nation and the world.

We saw an even more morally degraded "evangelical" voter bloc four years later in the 2016 election of our current President Donald J. Trump. Today, the term "evangelical" refers to a group that boldly embraces and accepts a profanity-using, thrice-married presidential candidate who stated he didn't need to ask God for forgiveness because "he's a good person." How can this be acceptable to Bible believers for the sake of political partisan support?

Many more pages and examples can be written on the irrelevance, weakness, and indifference of the local church. Unfortunately, the church at Laodicea describes the church of today. The Laodicean attitude of self-sufficiency prevails in the church today. We are comfortable on our campuses and in our sanctuaries, and we meld into the world when we leave. We have no standing in our communities because we have followed the big business model of American capitalism and provided ourselves a comfortable and isolated place to express our faith. The problem is, the majority of the time that we are active in our faith is when we are in our

66

sanctuaries. We have little or no desire to engage the world with our faith for the remainder of the week.

The church today, as was the church of Laodicea, is neither cold nor hot. It is not icy-cold, as is the world who has never heard the gospel. Nor is it fire-hot like a church that knows and accepts its rightful purpose in bringing Christ to the world. Rather, it is lukewarm. Having been forged by the grace of the gospel, we have now cooled down and become tepid, mainly due to our perceived self-sufficiency. We have forgotten that all we have comes from God. If this does not describe the current condition of the church, nothing does. Therefore, the Lord is preparing to spit us out of His mouth as something distasteful and downright repugnant. We can look around at our temporal and material possessions and conclude that the church knows how to get things done, has a wealth of knowledge, and financial strength. We appear to be blessed and favored by the Lord, but He sees us as ignorant and derelict of our fundamental mission in the world. To be clear, to be lukewarm is more distasteful than to be cold, and the disdain of our Lord will be equally distasteful.

What immediately follows the time of the Laodicean church is the rapture, the beginning of the tribulation and great tribulation, and the end of human history as it has been known. The church today is overweight, lazy, and irrelevant to the world for which it exists to save from the coming judgment. Because of our failures to fulfill the mission of evangelism, we are worthy of and awaiting judgment ourselves. It is estimated that between one-third and one-half of the billions on earth today have never heard the gospel of Jesus Christ. It appears the churchgoing population of the United States, now the smallest percentage of the population ever, is happy to sit in their sanctuaries and watch the world go to hell as we applaud and urge them on by the silence of our voices and the ignorance of our minds. We send checks to corporate offices to send missionaries to foreign and domestic fields, while the majority of American church members have never engaged the lost with a view of sharing the gospel. We have outsourced the Great Commission to a select few, and we have totally absolved ourselves of any personal responsibility to make disciples as we go through this life.

CHAPTER 14

BLESSED ARE THE DEAD
WHO DIE IN THE LORD

*And I heard a voice from heaven saying to me, Write, Blessed are
the dead which die in the Lord from now on: Yes, said the Spirit that
they may rest from their labors; and their works do follow them.*

—Revelation 14:13

The death of Donna was and is the sweetest and saltiest memory I possess. Sweet and salty has been a lifelong favorite taste combination of mine. The life, work, and death of this woman of God are the same on the spiritual palate. If I have ever had a living illustration of the above verse in my ministry, it was Donna. The works that followed her death were nothing short of miraculous and perhaps things that may never have occurred. "I must work the works of Him that sent me, while it is day: the night comes, when no man can work" (John 9:4).

When I arrived at this pastorate, I met Donna, her husband, and their or two daughters. The oldest daughter had a big, beautiful smile all the time. She would sing with the congregation, and her talent stood out. She was always too shy to do anything, especially sing before a group. When I would try to nudge her, her mother would say, "Oh, pastor, she is going to find her place one day. Then she will shine for the glory of the Lord Jesus

Christ." The youngest daughter was barely three or four. She was tiny, but she boasted the biggest, brightest radiance. They both were very close to their mom. Her husband was a special events type of churchgoer. Every time he came, we made a point of making him feel welcomed and loved. He was a very quiet man, a hard worker who worked many days while his family was in church. Donna would say every Sunday about her husband, "Pastor, let us just keep praying for him, because one day he is coming and he will keep coming."

The love of God and the light of Christ was the radiance in Donna's life. No matter the day, the time, or the place, these attributes were on display from this woman of God. In a church where there was so much wickedness in high places, a church where being rude with pungent attitudes was commonplace, this dear servant of God was a blessing and constant encouragement to her pastor and others. It was obvious from her conversation and her activities that bringing people to Christ and the church for discipleship was her only agenda. In the four or five years I knew Donna, she was responsible for more than eleven people being saved. Most of them were her family, and she would say, "Pastor, I got to get them all saved so we can have a family reunion in heaven one day." I was privileged to be involved in these spiritual transformations. For years, our church led in baptisms across our state for churches our size, and Donna was the direct cause. Life was not about her, it was about getting people to the King of Kings and the Lord of Lords. As I think over those years, Donna's life was a reenactment of the life of Philip. Philip was determined to seek out the lost, to bring them face-to-face with Jesus Christ, and then to be sure they were taught the precepts of the Word of God. Donna's life was a burning bush that was never consumed, a lily in the valley of disaster, a clear and concise form of communication from God to me saying, "You are where I want you, and doing what I called you here to do." No life in all my ministry shines with the glory of God as did the life of this dear woman.

How special was this follower of Christ? Only in heaven will we know. However, on earth she was an angel of the Lord. Donna, a nurse, was the first professional person of color to volunteer with a local mission's agency.

This organization created practical ministry and mission opportunities in inner-city communities, allowing Christians to engage the lost with a view towards evangelism. After twenty years of visiting and begging pastors and members from inner-city churches to help the poor, not one volunteer had come. The first one was Donna. Her life was a life well-lived. It seemed she knew, or at least sensed, that the night was coming and the day must be taken full advantage of, and so she did. She was the light of the world to many, the water from eternal wells for many a thirsty soul she met.

The news of her death came late one Thursday afternoon. Bible study the day before had been normal, except that Donna and I had discussed an illustration I had used the previous Sunday about flipping an old tractor. It was a narrow escape from severe injury or death. The point was that God takes care of His own, and he knows exactly when and where everything, including death, will occur for each of His children. It was typical for us to discuss biblical doctrine and theology. Donna was not a small talk person when it came to our conversations. She passed less than twenty-four hours later, in a violent automobile accident.

It was not until my wife and I were driving to be with her traumatized family that it occurred to me that our last conversation had been about the sovereignty of our God over death. Now, merely twenty-four hours later, she was absent from the body, but present with the Lord. The level of shock was unimaginable. It extended to the entire church family and our community, especially her husband and girls.

As I prepared to preach the Word of God in the form of a eulogy, I was so clearly led to a passage that spoke to one of the most overlooked or underrated truths and miracles of salvation. In John 8:51, Jesus says, "Verily, verily, I say unto you, if a man keeps my saying, he shall never see death." In the next verse, the Jews concluded that He, Jesus, was vexed with an evil spirit because of the statement in the preceding verse. This family was hurting because the loss was so mountainous, and also because of the violent nature of her death. The spirit of God pulled some Greek out of me that had not been used or thought of since my first year of Bible college. I was so amazed how God visibly, physically, emotionally, and spiritually used His word to calm the hearts of this grieving family. The question of why and how of her death is answered for the believer in this passage.

This nugget of truth is found in the Greek word translated in the King James Version as "see." The literal Greek definition or transliteration of the word means "to look at with interest and attention." In verse 52, the word "taste" is used by John similarly. The idea is that the believer will never be awestruck by the transition to death, no matter how it comes. The words of comfort for the family that day were, "Your sweet mother, wife, sister, and friend didn't feel, see, taste, experience, or pay attention to what was happening to her body in that moment. She saw the Savior, Jesus Christ, stepping out of the clouds and reaching down to pick her up and deliver her safely to His presence and that of our heavenly Father." Jesus is not saying here, as the Jews asserted, that the believer would live forever. He is saying, however, that the believer will die but the process of that death, no matter the form, will not be scary, dark, painful, or torturous because it is at that moment that the believer gets to see, touch, and taste the beauty and holiness of the Lord Jesus Christ.

What a calming word this was for all of us, and especially for that husband and those girls. I will never forget how that word seemed to take the bewilderment out of the hearts and minds of all of us there at such a heart-wrenching occasion. The Bible says that Jehovah is the God of all comfort and consolation. An overwhelming outpouring from the Comforter radically touched us all on that mournful day.

Moreover, on the isle of Patmos, John wrote these words, "And their works do follow after them." The work accomplished by Donna in the flesh and on earth was equivalent to "dust on the butcher scales." Although her work for the Lord on earth was gigantic in quantity, the work that God did after her death was and is a testimony of her faithfulness to the Great Commission: "As you go, make disciples" (my paraphrase of the literal translation of the Greek phrase in Matt. 28:19a). Her devotion to leading people to the Lord for salvation was unmitigated. To illustrate this, I will focus on the three people in her immediate family. In the beginning of this chapter, I mentioned the church attendance of her husband. It has been ten years since that awful day, and I dare say that her husband has not missed ten Sunday worships. At first, he would come in with his girls and leave as soon as worship was over. He never spoke unless spoken to and sat with a sad countenance. He remains a very quiet and humble man, but he has become a giant in our church family. He enters into conversation, claps his hands, sings to the music, and serves as a deacon and financial officer. His wife knew years before that this would occur, and her works followed her.

The oldest daughter, now twenty-four and full of life, has led our interpretive dance ministry for several years. She creates the dances and choreographs the moves to the music. She selects the songs, and they are always appropriate and anointed. She gives leadership to teens. She is an amazing young woman who also is in worship consistently. So many other positive attributes are left unsaid. She lives a beautiful life, one of which her mother would be proud.

Now the youngest daughter is a junior in college preparing for medical school. No doubt another influence of her mother, who was a nurse. What I've seen God do in the life of this little girl, now a young lady, has eternally impacted my heart and hers. She read a letter or poem she had written at her mother's funeral. It tore me up emotionally; I was about to preach, and I wondered if I could get through the service without breaking down totally. She stood at the edge of the pulpit just a few inches above the casket in which her mother's remains rested. Like a lion, she got through her reading like a champion of the Lord. God strengthened me for my responsibility by the courage of that little girl. She, too, was consistently in the church until she left for college.

As I conclude this section, I remember their smiles; smiles that God created. Each of these three dear people went through one of the saddest, most urgent changes of life, and it naturally left them sad. The spirit of God, on more than one occasion, led me to preach to that family. One was a series of sermons focused on Revelation and the present state of those saints who are already in heaven. Through those twelve sermons, I saw smiles begin to appear and the twinkle that only hope and understanding can create.

When the youngest daughter was in ninth or tenth grade, the spirit of God told me to take the teens on a trip far away, an adventure in new territory, with a new mission. I took them to New York City. As we left the church, the youngest daughter was sitting on a bench in the van such that I could see her in the rearview mirror. The Lord said to me, "This trip is for her. Her sadness will turn to a permanent smile, and she will be well after this trip." Before that trip was over, I observed a complete metamorphosis in her emotional psyche. More than five years have passed since that trip and her smile is permanent. The hope and the intrinsic fortitude in her life are well-established by the Scripture and the spirit of Almighty God.

CHAPTER 15

GOD SPEAKS CLEARLY: LET THE PROPERTY GO

And thine ears shall hear a word behind thee, saying,
This is the way, walk ye in it, when ye turn to the right hand,
and when ye turn to the left.

—Isaiah 30:21

I was impressed, while flying home from a fourteen-day mission trip to African countries, by the spirit of God to sell our church property and rent or lease space in one of the thousands of underused church properties in our city. Understanding fully that this is not what Baptists do, I immediately felt I would be voted out. The building was built and financed before my tenure began. I inherited a building built on the cheap, with all sorts of issues, the least of which was not the $300,000 mortgage. A storm came through our town in the late nineties, and the frame of the new church was destroyed. The entire frame of this new edifice was torn down, and the church had to begin the work of building a new church again. I read the article in the paper, drove by the location, and visually observed the damage. At this point, I knew nothing about this church and knew even less about God's plan to call me there in a couple of years. Due to the lack of correct supervision of the work and efforts to save money, this church spent too much on a sanctuary that seated 180, but with a parking lot for only forty cars. From the outside, the place looked packed, and visitors kept coming, but in reality, the place was only a third filled. After I arrived as pastor, the congregation was left with a huge monthly mortgage and no money for missions and ministry. Also, we were in a blighted neighborhood where we earnestly tried to serve the lost, but we were constantly robbed by the folk we were trying to serve. For instance, our $28,000 HVAC system was destroyed twice in a three-year period for a few dollars of copper. Additionally, cars were stolen and broken into while we worshipped. Therefore, in an attempt to stop the carnage, we paid over $1,200 a month for outdoor lighting.

In 2005, I went to Ecuador to facilitate the planting of a training center for native pastors and lay leaders. I was the guest of a missionary couple who had served many years in Togo prior to coming to South America. This couple gave me an African carving of an African queen that had on a tiara and a necklace. I love woodcarvings; I took it home and placed it in my office. For six years, it was the source of many conversations. In 2010, on my first trip to Togo, I learned that this part of Africa, similar to Haiti, was a headquarters for voodoo and black magic. On my third trip to Togo, I went to the Temple of the Python to observe this unbelievably idolatrous phenomenon. Yes, a church where a snake is an idol. My interpreter told me that during the gathering of slaves by the Portuguese, witch doctors and others considered to be demon-possessed people were taken to a place to attempt to beat or starve the evil out of them before placing them on the ships. In that place, there arose very heavy worship of idols, and the python snake became the main god of the idolaters. Days later, on the flight home, the spirit of the Lord spoke to me clearly saying, "Upon arrival at home, examine the carving in your office." So, perturbed by the urging, upon landing in Atlanta after twenty-six hours of travel, I drove to Augusta, passed my home, and proceeded to my office to examine this carving I had been housing for years. As I entered my office and examined the carving, I noticed immediately that the necklace was snake heads connected to each other, and the tiara on the head was snake heads standing up to form the spires or peaks. I was stunned and scared by this carving, which was promoting the false god of the Temple of the Python. I did not need any more instructions, I knew exactly what to do. I collected the carving and headed home. Upon arriving, I gathered some firewood, started a fire, and burned it. Afterward, I put water on the ashes, placed them in a bag, and carried them to a commercial dumpster so as not to leave even the remnant of its ashes on my property.

After all this was done, and I was unpacking and settling in, the spirit of the Lord said to me, "I want you to do the same with the church property. Get rid of it so that these people are not associated with it ever again, in any way." In January 2011, I presented this idea to the church. I shared with them about the carving and how it was dedicated and carved in honor of a false god. I told them how God instructed me to remove it completely from my possession. I told them that is exactly what God now wants us to do with this church property. Internally, I was thinking this would be my final business meeting. I did not think the people would understand this concept as God's agenda and progressive for the kingdom of God. I gave the congregation two weeks to pray, think on this matter, and to ask questions. Not one person called, emailed, or texted with a question. I took that as an indication that I would be voted out.

Two weeks later when it was time to vote on the matter of dispossessing ourselves of this property, the sanctuary was full, and it was almost a unanimous vote to move, except for two members who felt the building was irreplaceable. Many comments were made in support of the move. I was shocked and relieved, as I could see the hand of God speaking to His people through the consistent teaching of His word. I saw a spiritual maturity in these people, and I was greatly encouraged by their decision. Within a month, we settled into a new location, sharing space in a declining church.

Moreover, within six months we closed on the property, selling it to another church. I must add that I did a full disclosure to the purchasing church; the poor construction, the too-small parking lot, the thefts, and the cost to service the debt. I never shall forget the day of the closing when I called the pastor and congratulated him on the closing. His words to me were, "Pastor, this purchase has almost destroyed my church. We have a building, but our congregation has been torn up over the course of obtaining it."

The issue was twofold, as I look back. God's people were cheerfully and willing giving their earnings to the Lord, but the bank, the power company, and others were getting nearly eighty cents out of every dollar. The other issue was the property itself. After we moved, our congregation had peace and harmony that we had not experienced before. So much so that I was preaching at a mission's conference and shared with the pastor that my church was having a business meeting in my absence. His eyes bucked, his face cringed with disbelief, and with a raised voice, he asked, "And you are not there?" He went on to say he would never allow his church to have a business meeting without him, "Because you never know what will happen in those meetings!" I went on to explain to him how our meetings are never unpredictable because the goal is the glory of God and no one is looking for anything but the will of God. When God points out something or someone that He wants you to separate from, you should do it because it is always for your good and His glory.

CHAPTER 16

THE CALL TO MINISTRY
IS NOT ALWAYS A CALL TO THE PULPIT

As you go, make disciples.

—Matthew 28:20
(my paraphrase of the literal translation of the Greek)

Ellis was a preacher and an employee of the state detention center for juvenile offenders. His passion for sharing the gospel was obvious, and he was looking for a church to call him as pastor so that he could resign his state job. Ellis did not rest until he was called to a small rural church. With merely a calling and great passion for leading God's people, he went to that church and immediately began to experience that which he never thought possible. It was a Missionary Baptist church where the traditional leadership is deacons and trustees (trustees not in the sense of corporate officers, which states require, but as in overseers of financial and business matters of the church). After his first sermon, he was instructed that preaching on sin was not permitted. Their reason was, "We are all saints and have left the ways of darkness, so we have no need to be preached to about sin."

This small rural church met on second and fourth Sundays only. On Ellis's second Sunday, he preached on the topic of tithe and offering as God's appointed method for financing the work of ministry through the church. After worship, another leader approached him and said, "This is a New Testament church, and we do not ascribe to the tithe and offering as presented in the Old Testament because it is outdated, and we have fundraisers periodically to cover our needs." It was then that he reached out to me to share his experience from his first two Sundays and sought advice for what to preach. My advice was to preach the Word of God, regardless of what they wanted or did not want to hear. And so that is what he did for the next two months. On his sixth Sunday, the leadership called a meeting before the benediction to hold a vote of confidence which was not in his favor. That was his last Sunday at that church.

He came to me defeated by what happened, how it happened, and why it happened. He said he felt as though he had missed God's instruction on that church but knew, without a doubt, that God had called him to ministry. It was then that I was able to show him that God had indeed called him to ministry, but his calling should not be limited to a pulpit. He did not understand because preaching, in his Christian experience, had always been connected to a pulpit. This brother and I became very close friends, and we are, to this day, very close.

I used his secular employment to show him that a pulpit is anywhere someone can hear the gospel. I instructed him not to limit God's work through him to a specific place and time but to see the youth he served every day as the parishioners that God had called him to preach. As a result of this advice, my brother began to share his faith and show the love of Christ to the boys in his care. He rose to management positions in that organization and led many young men and women to the Lord. He never pastored again, but he never stopped preaching. There are juvenile murderers, rapists, and burglars who came to Christ because of Ellis. He learned to make disciples as he went about his daily routine.

Additionally, he created ways for faith groups to come into the center to serve the teens and hold worship. Thousands of young people heard the gospel and hundreds were saved, leaving the center changed eternally. No one knows how many people were touched as a result of Ellis's ministry. One thing is for sure; God calls us to make disciples as we go, not as they come to a church. Our world would be a different and better place if more men and women could grasp that their calling is not limited to a pulpit but is something they can engage in wherever God has placed them in the workforce.

Recently, Ellis shared with me a letter from a man who was a child in the facility years ago. The man shared in the letter how angry he was at that point in his life. He had learned to cope with people by displaying raging anger towards those he was intimidated by or with whom he did not wish to deal. He stated, "My anger was used to make people back away from me and leave me to myself. It worked on every staff person in the facility except you, Mr. Ellis. For some reason, you did not back away, and you were always patient and loving towards me even when I said and did mean things. I am now in a technical college and preparing to complete a certificate in automotive repair. I have a job, and I am getting married to the mother of my son next month. Your words changed my life. I accepted Christ because of you, and I wrote this to say thank you for being my preacher when you didn't know you were being that to me."

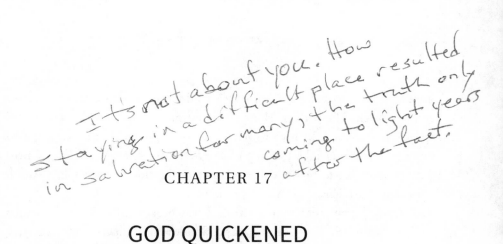

It's not about you. How staying in a difficult place resulted in salvation for many, the truth only coming to light years after the fact.

CHAPTER 17

GOD QUICKENED
WHEN I WANTED TO QUIT

Sister Ethel

Be ye steadfast and unmovable,
always abounding in the work of the Lord.

—I Corinthians 15:58

I wanted to quit many times during the first seven years of my ministry at one particular church. The reality I faced in that church was not the idea I had from the beginning, and it was not working out well from my perspective. The majority of the people were thankless, and they were darkness-dwellers. This church provided, by far, the hardest, most severe battles with the enemy I had ever endured. Spiked with fiery darts from the enemy and his imps, these were the most difficult years of my ministry. At times, there were constant attacks from the enemy, often through people who I had come to trust. I wanted to quit, and each time I was close to exercising that option, God would show me why I could not. He would show me why I had to remain in His utility.

At the interview meeting, the church held to get acquainted with their potential new pastor, there was no small amount of discord and division. These people did not like each other, and they were trying to decide if they could or would like me as their new pastor. After answering a few questions about methodology, I was asked how I would deal with the different factions in the church. The person asking the question pointed out that the church was deeply divided. In my answer, I told them that I would not side with anyone, but rather take the side of the Scripture, the side of Jesus Christ. Anyone wanting to be on a side other than the side of Jesus Christ would choose to side against Him and not me.

Immediately after that meeting, I was beckoned by a senior woman sitting to my left. Her face was impossible to read during the meeting, so I was dealing with some trepidation as I went to her. She and her husband were seated, so I leaned down to her and she took the lapel of my suit, pulled me closer, and said, "Pastor, I'm on God's side, too!" From that moment and until God called her home at age ninety-two , she was my friend and encourager when things were dark and when they were bright. She was my angel of the Lord.

I remember calling her from Romania while on a mission trip to talk about some of the issues in the church. She was so delighted that I would call and talk to her from such a long distance. The issue was about a woman in the church who was generating discord and creating another schism. This dear sister counseled me, prayed with me, and advised me on how to handle the situation. I did as she said, and the problem was resolved without incident. I would rather have one woman like this praying for me than any number of associate pastors sitting in the pulpit.

The only time the dissenting crowd returned to the church, after being dispossessed of leadership on my first day as pastor, was when the judge required us to have a second vote. This group had wreaked havoc on my character and that of the church. Also, on this day, they stood around the walls staring at me, rather than sitting. They had the unmitigated gall to think that they had a stake in a church that they had done nothing for in almost six months. What, but pride germinated by biblical ignorance, could give a person the impression that God is accepting of such behavior? After the sermon, which was entitled "Killing Giants That Prevent Spiritual Growth," someone began to sing the hymn by Fredrick Whitfield entitled, "Oh, How I Love Jesus." The voice of the person leading the song was

Dr. Gilbert to the rescue

purely alto, and so I looked for the man who was leading. As it turned out it was Sister Ethel. Oh, how this song blessed my soul and strengthened me for the road ahead.

Many times during my quiet time, I would recall how the first line of that hymn was a tranquilizer to my soul. "There is a name I love to hear; I love to sing its worth; it sounds like music in mine ear, the sweetest name on earth." Ethel is in heaven now, singing around the throne of God. Nevertheless, I can still hear her voice speaking directly to my heart on that day through the words of that song. In the midst of the blackest darkness, the Lord sent a lamp unto my feet and a light unto my path through this dear woman of God.

I am convinced that she is one of heaven's chosen that God sent me there to rescue. I was with her through the deaths of her husband, son, and grandson. I could never repay this woman of God for how she quietly ministered to me so consistently for the thirteen years I served as her pastor. So many Sundays when I was weary in the work, she would say to me, "Pastor, I know they say this is incorrect English, but I declare in Jesus' name that the message of God through you just keeps getting gooder and gooder!" She went on many times to mention the need for more Bible education in the church.

She was my personal "angel of the Lord" as I followed the call of God. There are times in the life of every believer when he or she feels alone. Also, there are times that test our physical and emotional ability to keep giving of one's self. In these times, the sacrifice seems excessive. Every believer needs an angel of the Lord to wipe the tears from his or her heart and eyes. I am not discounting the presence of God the Spirit, the Lord Jesus Christ. Nevertheless, sometimes we need someone in the flesh who embodies the Lord "localized" with us. It is through the presence of these special operatives of the Lord, such as Ethel, that God chooses to inform believers that they are where God wants them to be and everything will be all right.

In Genesis 22, God tells Abraham to go to the mountain to worship and sacrifice his only son; what a lot to ask of a man. This man had previously left his country, his culture, and his kinfolk for the Word of God. This story is one of the sweetest of stories of how God always gives the believer assurance of His presence, power, and provision. Being confronted by an angel of the Lord is what Jamieson, Brown, and Fausset call an "occasion for the development of his faith.[1]"

Abraham was assured all was well and would remain so. This story begins and ends with an angel of the Lord. Everywhere God has sent me, he has also sent an angel of the Lord to keep me company, to be a friend at my side.

Sister Ethel was that for me in this church. So often, she prayed, shouted, and spoke words of God to me so that I would not be distracted by what the church was going through and lose the focus of where we were going. Even from her hospital bed, she would take hold of my hand or my necktie, which was her preference, and pull me closer to her. It was during those times she spoke life, hope, and purpose into my weary soul. She did that until the Lord called her home. On the day the nurses removed the life support systems from her (she would pass a couple of days later), I, along with her family had worship at her bedside. We sang, prayed, and praised her God, our God—Jehovah. It was a mountaintop experience. I have had many great worship experiences, but that day was indeed one of the sweetest.

 I would contend that if any minister, missionary, layman, or regular believer is wondering whether or not they are in the will of God, look for an angel of the Lord. The absence of one indicates one is off course. God sent an angel of the Lord not only to Abraham but also to Hagar, Jacob, Moses, and others. He will send an angel of the Lord to you as well. In this church, he sent me Sister Ethel, and just as Moses experienced on the mountain, I was encouraged and spiritually fed through her prayers, touch, words, facial expressions, raised eyebrow, songs, shouts, and laughs. This woman taught me more than seminary and Bible college ever did, that God is with us.

---

1   Robert Jamieson, David Brown, and A. R. Fausset, *A Commentary, Critical and Explanatory, on the Whole Bible—Vol. 1 Genesis-Deuteronomy* (Hendrickson Publishers, 2002), 173.

Dr Gilbert to the rescue + the providence of God.

Another attack was about four years into this pastorate. At the time, there was little indication that the evil, which had been allowed to fester through biblical ignorance, was subsiding. There were all sorts of fires related to personal pride and pursuits by people with the need to be seen, heard, respected, and idolized by the remainder of the congregation. This lesson began during a Wednesday night discipleship as we discussed details for the upcoming musical. One of the chief instigators of trouble and a hater of contentment was irritated and created a big fuss about a very insignificant matter: the color of the choir outfits. After I had exhausted every means possible to answer, respect, and appease this woman, I decided I was just about ready to give her a piece of my mind.

My younger brother, having known me all his life, was there that night and could see the transition taking place within me. He made his way to the front and whispered in my ear that this woman was not worth ruining my ministry. Those words brought me back to reality, and God's spirit took control of my anger. (See chapter "Proof That the Grace of God Had Changed My Life.") However, as I fumed over this event for the remainder of the week, I wanted to quit. I was ready and told God I would go to the deepest darkest jungle to serve Him, but I was tired of these stiff-necked people. God waited until Sunday evening to acknowledge my request for release from this church.

On the Sunday evening of the concert, my wife and I arrived a little early. As we pulled up, another car immediately pulled in next to us with a mixed-race couple in it. They were lost and looking for a shopping area that was nowhere near where we were. They were very friendly and amiable. We gave them directions and invited them to stay for the musical. They did and enjoyed our fellowship so much that they came back on Wednesday and the following Sunday. On the second Wednesday of their attendance, I was able to lead the man to Christ. There are many interesting facts about this situation. First, we only had this musical worship once a month on Sunday evenings, so for them to get lost and end up in our parking lot was not a coincidence. Secondly, the wife was already a Christian, but the husband was of Italian and Iranian heritage. This young man had previously practiced only Islam as his religion. Thirdly, God spoke to me the instant that this man accepted Christ and told me that, had I left this church as I wanted to, I would not have been able to lead this man to Him. This act of salvation, arranged by the spirit of God, was miraculous in the life of this young man. If the story ended here, it would not be miraculous.

This young man lost his paternal family when he professed Jesus as his Savior, and I became his father, his brother, and his friend. This couple ended up being transferred to New England because the wife was a high-ranking army officer. After the move, we stayed in touch, and I still prayed for and counseled him on a regular basis. This young convert went on to become a secret service member and served many high-ranking government officials, including former Presidents Clinton and Obama. He has shared his faith and his walk with God, and God has blessed him and carried him through many difficult times. To this day, he is a faithful believer with a young family. Repeatedly, the spirit of God has reminded me that had I moved on my volition to leave the church, this witness would not exist. This soul would not be saved. This life would not be his. This pastorate was hard, but years later when I was made aware of this young man's evangelism, I accepted that even though God often calls us to hard places, He is there with us at all times.

SECTION THREE

RACISTS ARE IN THE CHURCH
BUT NONE ARE IN CHRISTIANITY

CHAPTER 18

Babel, the beginning of races.

RACISM AND ITS INCEPTION INTO THE HUMAN RACE

... and from there did the Lord scatter them abroad on the face of all the earth.

—Genesis 11

With the confounding of the languages came some other divisions in the human race which created stark differences and dividers between humans. The human race, until then, had been united and shared the same language and general location. The desire of man to approach God Jehovah on man's terms rather than the terms specified by God Himself has always been an issue for the unregenerate man.

The idea of strength in numbers is obvious here. God declares that because man shared a common language, their collective imagination would stop at nothing their sin nature desired. This led to another worldwide condition; that which led to the Noahic flood in Genesis 6:5. In essence, the confounding or confusing of the languages of man was necessary in the scheme of God to develop a permanent plan of salvation. As a result of the languages being confused, people began to scatter across the globe. It is this that created the different ethnicities and skin hues (what we call "races" today). It must be stated at this point that, biblically, there is but one race,

Sudan

which is the human race, and it is divided only into classes of people, Jews, and Gentiles, or saved and lost. Racism is a sin issue, not a skin issue.

I was in South Sudan, some 8,000 miles from home, when the spirit of the Lord taught me this lesson: racism, racial prejudice, and all similar issues are rooted in sin. I met some of the dearest men and women of God in the city of Malakal, Sudan. These brothers and sisters were distraught over the many years, indeed decades, of civil war in their country. As we sat over lunch during our midday break from the Bible training I was leading, I began to drill down on the reasons for the war and its ravages on their lives. Sudan is a country where parents, to this day, mark the faces of their children by cutting tribal symbols to distinguish them from other tribes. When I asked why there was so much hatred of each other across the tribes, the answer became clear. Some tribes think they are superior to others, and so they wage war with the intent of destroying the inferior tribes. I listened to the stories of how neighbors would not allow neighbors to raise chickens or grow crops with the hope of starving them to death. I heard how most of these tribesmen in my class had never ventured more than a mile from the place of their birth, and how systematically one tribe would hunt others with the purpose of maiming, raping, and consummately destroying it. I was taken aback by the fact that all these tribal people looked alike.

Their skin tone, their hair texture, their lack of means, and their living conditions were identical, yet they hated each other as though there were differences. This hatred was not light skin against dark skin, straight hair against curly hair; they all looked and lived the same, and yet they hated one another. I dare say they hated each other with the same passion with which some whites in the United States hate blacks and vice versa. It was here that the Lord showed me that the issue was in the heart, not in the hue of the skin. In other places around the world, I have observed the same inferior versus superior mindset among different people groups with similar physical features. In Eastern Europe, where I have spent more than two decades working among the Roma, the same racist attitudes and practices exist. Romanians, Hungarians, and the Roma, or Gypsy people, have coexisted for generations, but the Roma are as discriminated against

Ȟ: Romania

and ostracized today as people of color were in the United States at the height of the Jim Crow era. These three people groups also share the same physical characteristics, but racism is alive and well among them. The Hungarians view themselves as superior to the Romanians, the Romanians view themselves as superior to the Hungarians, and they both hate and disdain the Roma people. In 2012, the Lord led me and my missionary in Romania to host a citywide revival in a small town where all three groups lived. This gathering constituted the first time that Christians from these groups would be worshipping the Lord together. I saw the Lord high and lifted up in that cultural house one very cold winter evening in Șimleu Silvaniei, a town in Sălaj County, of Transylvania, Romania.

Preaching to about seven hundred people with all three ethnicities present, I asked the Lord to show me if what I was doing was acceptable to Him and if He was using me in any tangible way. Mission trips are hard on me for many reasons. The main one being that I fast the majority of the time with absolutely no intake of meats and fresh vegetables. This goes without mentioning the hardship of being away from family and local ministry. I wanted to know if I was enduring these tough times for the good of the Kingdom of God. God used my observations in this worship service to answer my question.

Preaching through an interpreter, one has pauses that allow for observation that normally don't exist. It was during one of the breaks in the message that evening that I asked the above question of the Lord. As I did, I immediately noticed a Romanian lady sitting to my left on the very front row of this packed auditorium. This lady had her toddler son sitting in the seat next to her.

This Romanian mother and believer from the First Baptist Church of Șimleu made her son sit in her lap, then began to beckon for someone to my right to come and take the seat. This went on for several minutes and I soon realized that she was trying to get an elderly Roma lady, clad in her traditional garb, to come and take the seat. I noticed there was reluctance on the part of the Roma lady. The Roma customarily took their places in the balcony and at the rear of the room, as people of color would have done during the time of racial segregation in the United States. Many people, such as the elderly woman, simply stood in the doorway to hear the gospel.

The Romanian Christian did not relent and continued to beckon the elderly Roma to the seat for what seemed like an eternity. Finally, the old woman slowly made short and hesitant steps across the front of that packed room to the seat. As she walked over, I could feel a collective pause in the room. A gasp could be felt and heard as this Roma lady made her way to the front row to be seated between those who had personally and institutionally expressed their superiority over her. Once she made it to the seat, it felt as though the room exhaled. The Roma people were obviously expecting humiliation, and the Hungarians and Romanians were astonished by what was happening as much as I was. Up to this point, the room had been positively gelid, but after the Roma lady sat down and was hugged by the Romanian believer who had invited her over, the spiritual temperature in the room was elevated to unreal levels, and the spirit of the Lord descended upon our meeting in a powerful way.

That evening, Hungarians, Romanians, and Roma believers hugged, cried, prayed, and praised the Lord Jesus Christ together for the first time, and the Lord whispered to my spirit that, yes, I was where He wanted me, doing what he willed me to do, and that the menial inconveniences were sacrifices for the expansion of the kingdom of God. God said to me that the seating of this lady was tantamount to me being ushered in and seated in the front row of any white church in the "Deep South" during segregation. I will never forget that lesson and the fact that, except for the clothing, you could not differentiate between the three ethnicities based on skin or hair. The Bible clearly teaches that God is no respecter of persons (Romans 2:11) and that believers should not judge based on physical appearances (John 7:24).

Indubitably, one will ascertain from the Word of God that racism is a sin which is not compatible with Christianity. One cannot love God whom he has not seen and hate his brother who lives next door. This scourge upon the church is worldwide, but particularly in America, and has been allowed to hang around and stain the witness of the church, rendering her less effective in being light and salt to a dark and dying world.

In his book, *Purging Racism from Christianity*, Jefferson D. Edwards quotes King David: "Redeem me from the oppression of men, that I may obey your precepts" (Psalm 119:134 NIV). He adds, "This scripture implies that as long as I am under the oppression of men, it will be hard for me to obey the Lord's precepts and purposes." He goes on to say that the church, in large part, has not challenged oppressive systems, choosing to coexist with them and ignore one of Christ's major commissions—to liberate, deliver, and free the poor and the oppressed.

I attended seminary for my Master of Divinity degree in Memphis, Tennessee, the place where Martin Luther King Jr. was assassinated. It was in this city of Dr. King's assignation that I discovered that the road of racism is integrated, because blacks and whites travel it equally. It was here I was told, "You aren't black enough to serve in my church since you are attending a school led by and designed for white folks." Yet it was in this city, as a direct result of the ultra-racist tone and tenor of churches of color, that I was led to worship across racial lines. It was here I began to see that the only color that mattered to God was the rich-red, royal blood of Christ who died for all humanity. It was in this city that I introduced my wife and daughter to multiethnic fellowships at which the love of God ruled in the hearts of men. It was in this city that the Lord taught me that my calling was to men, regardless of their skin color. And it was in this city that I came to know that one can be a racist and a church member, but you can't be a racist and a Christian.

CHAPTER 19

Babel, racism, and Acts 2 and the
end of the
SALVATION IS THE ANTIDOTE
curse of
FOR THE POISON OF BABEL
Babel.

And it shall come to pass, that whoever shall call
on the name of the Lord shall be saved.

—Acts 2:21

In the chapter related to racism, we discussed the Tower of Babel and the impact of the concerted sin of the world, along with God's response to that sin. In this chapter, our goal is to present and explore the day of Pentecost as the antidote for racism and division among believers. The curse of Babel remains as active as ever among the nonbeliever. It cannot be dealt with by legislation or civil and human rights. It is a sin of the heart, with the only cure being the indwelling of the Holy Spirit. As Acts 2 opens, the believers are unified. After all that has occurred, including the different responses to the crucifixion, the disciples were of one accord. Unity is a hallmark of the New Testament church.

Many believers and scholars have hung themselves up on the rushing wind and the tongues of fire, missing what I contend to be the greatest miracle in the chapter. Since so much has been made of those occurrences, I will not linger there, but move on to the filling of the Holy Ghost. This spiritual indwelling provides a cure for the poison of Babel. Without His presence in one's life, the natural, cultural, and historical tendency of every man is to be racist and carry a sense of inherent superiority over others. In America, it is based on skin color. In Africa, it is based on tribes. In India, it is based on caste. It is a sin housed in every unregenerate heart. Only the blood of Jesus Christ can cure this.

Acts Chapter 2 contains a multitude of miracles. The miracle of tongues or languages is the most discussed one, but it should be noted how many barriers are removed, how many illegitimate divisions are closed, and how many doors are opened to believers, be they young, old, male, or female. In Verses 8-11 the curse of Babel, as it relates to languages, is reversed. This also proffers the miracle of understanding and speaking of unlearned languages or tongues. The prophecy of Joel is induced in Verses 16-18, and these verses begin the tearing down of the divisions of Babel. It is here we see that all the divisions men still prop up in society and church are removed from the New Testament church. The spirit of the Lord is poured out on all flesh—all believing flesh, that is. The spirit of the Lord is poured upon young males and females, older women and older men, on male and female slaves.

No New Testament church can rightfully deny the above genders, stations, and ages of people the ability or opportunity to be used by the Lord for His glory and the growth of the church. This is the antidote for the Babel poison: the Holy Spirit of the Lord Jesus Christ. I contend the church has been stymied because she has not allowed many to serve based on ill-conceived barriers and divisions. She has also been stymied because of her refusal to take a stand and speak the truth of the Word of God to the world concerning this sin.

A seminary professor was once asked how he dealt with the civil rights movement and the coming of people of color to his Southern Baptist church in West Memphis, Arkansas. His reply was, "I was told that we might have protesters visit us on the coming Sunday, so I called a meeting of my deacons and informed them that our strategy would be to say nothing for fear of creating a scene and having our church in the national news. I had the deacons inform all the ushers that they were to say nothing to the protesters, just let them come in and have a seat." Then he said, "I told them that I would say nothing to them or about them and, hopefully, they will leave and never come back." This is typical of how white Christians dealt with this issue. In churches of color, the civil rights movement was born and nurtured. In fact, this movement took over the church for decades and, in some cases, remains the rallying cry for many.

There is no cure for racism except the work of the Holy Spirit in the heart of believers. There is no black or white Jesus. At best, He is olive and can be defined as a combination of all skin hues. The book of the Revelation makes it abundantly clear that around the throne of God in heaven will be people from every nation, tribe, and tongue. The greatest miracle in Acts 2 is the unity of the believers across racial, denominational, geographic, and language barriers. The world has been poisoned by this sin of racism. The antidote came in form of the Holy Spirit. Have you received the antidote?

CHAPTER 20

Mr. James gets the last word.

SPEAKING AGAINST RACISM
FROM THE GRAVE

We know that we have passed from death to life, because we love the brothers. He that loves not his brother stays in death.

—John 3:14

One of the godliest men God has allowed me to meet is James Macy. Mr. James was a safety engineer for a power company. He was a man who loved the Lord, studied the Bible, and wedded his spiritual understanding with the practical everyday application of those truths. In addition, true to the term "James of all trades," Mr. James could fix, build, restore, or repair almost anything. He was a collector of guns, knives, unusual wood pieces, antique power meters, and classic automobiles. He was a family man, a godly man with a heart for missions, and he was retired when we met him around 1995.

Mr. James was in his late 60s when we became church members and friends. He was very attracted to expository preaching, and that was the basis for our fast and strong friendship. Many times, we discussed Bible passages, principles, or one of my recent sermons. These conversations took place mostly in his den, garage, or workshop where I admired his collections. During one of these occasions, Mr. James asked me to promise him that I would preach his funeral. I was shocked by this request for we had not known each other very long. In addition, the fact that there were other preachers in his life with whom he had much longer relationships left me puzzled. I consented, but in my mind that was an event in the distant future and nothing to focus on anytime soon.

In the mid-to-late nineties, I did much preaching at Promise Keeper rallies, at individual churches, and in small rural cities throughout the southeastern United States. God used me to preach a racial reconciliation message titled "You Can Be a Racist and a Church Member, but You Can't Be a Racist and a Christian." I think it was that message that prompted my good friend to make his request. We had many very frank discussions about this issue; how it affected the Georgia he grew up in, how it played out on a job when people of color were hired, and when they were allowed to bid for jobs historically held only by whites.

I preached this message dozens of times in a five-year period. I recall preaching this in Wrightsville, GA in a series of messages focused on the need for the church to awaken to the fact that we are the only institution on earth with the power to fix this issue. On the last night of this community-wide rally held in a tent on the high school football field, a man I later learned to be a racist associated with the KKK came to the worship and stood in the center aisle, staring at me for what seemed like an eternity. With an escort to the county line, I made my exit that evening. Mr. James often mentioned his friends and coworkers and how they felt about the legitimacy of racial disparities. Often, he told me how his friends disagreed with him on this issue.

Early in March of 2009, I received the call from his dear wife that Mr. James had gone to be with Jesus. She asked if I was still willing and able to fulfill my promise to deliver the eulogy. Mr. James had developed Parkinson's disease, and they had moved closer to their children so that his wife would have help when needed. This was a part of rural Georgia, which may be characterized as having a 1950s mindset as it relates to race relations. When I arrived at the church on the day of the funeral, I went in to meet the pastor. The look on his face, the blood-red tint from the neck up, told me that Mr. James had not told them I was a man of color. Once he was over the initial shock, he greeted me and said, "You gonna make history today. You will be the first person of color to enter this pulpit, and perhaps this church." It was at that point that I knew Mr. James had one last message for his friends.

The pallbearers and the church leadership were all in their mid-seventies, and they knew a world devoid of anyone of color having authority over them and definitely not leading in any worship of which they were a part. When they walked in and saw me in the pulpit, they looked like they thought, "That James has brought up this issue again." I preached the cross of Christ and shared the plan of salvation as Mr. James had requested. During the entirety of the service, Mr. James' male friends turned their bodies in their seats so as not to be facing the pulpit as I preached. At first, I felt awkward but then quickly realized this was something God had orchestrated with Mr. James. He wanted these people to be confronted by the truth of the gospel for perhaps their last time. He wanted them to hear it from a man of color. They never made eye contact, never looked toward the front of the church, and at the cemetery, they never said a word to me. They were uncomfortable and seemed aggravated that Mr. James had gotten the last word in, even from the grave.

I do not know if I have ever seen any of those men again, but I do know that they heard the gospel that day. I further stated in that eulogy that if they did not accept the Christ of the gospel they heard, they would never see their friend James Lacy again, because he was in heaven, and no one gets to heaven while hating his brother.

SEVEN EXPOSITORY SERMON OUTLINES

JESUS IS OUR HIDING PLACE (Josh. 20:1-9; Ps. 32:7)
  I.   The Appointment of the Cities (vv.1-3)
  II.   The Admittance to the City (vv. 4, 9)
  III. The Action of the City (v. 5)
  IV.   The Absence from the City (vv. 6-9)

HOW TO STOP THE PLAGUE (2 Sam. 24:17-25)
  I.   Confess Prayerfully (vv. 17-18)
  II.   Commit Personally (vv. 19-23, 25)
  III. Certain Price /Cash Purchase (v. 24)

INSTRUCTIONS FOR MINISTRY (I Sam. 8)
  I.   The Summons (vv. 1-11)
  II.   The Sermon (vv. 12-21)
  III. The Supplication (vv. 22-53)
  IV.   The Servant's Sure Promises (vv. 54-61)
  V.   The Sacrifices (vv. 62-66)

JOHN THE BAPTIST (Luke 1:18-20; 57-64; 67-80)
  I.   The Blindness That Leads to Dumbness (vv. 18-20)
  II.   The Burden That Leads to Delivery (vv. 57-64)
  III. The Blood That Leads to Deliverance (vv. 67-80)

REQUIRED READING FROM RUTH (Ruth 1:1-4:17)
  I.   In the Worst of Times, God Will See You Through
       (Ruth 1:1-5)
  II. No One Is Ever Too Far from the Reach of God
       (Ruth 1:14-18)
  III. God Guides Those Who Desire to Follow Him and Serve
       Others (Ruth 2:1-3)
  IV. There Are No Small Decisions with God (Ruth 2:4-12)
  V.   It Pays to Wait on the Lord to Work Things Out
       (Ruth 2:22; 3:18; 4:17)

GREATER HEIGHTS OF KINGDOM BUILDING (Hag. 1-2)
  I.   A Bag with Holes (Hag. 1:3-9; Matt. 6:33 (Hands)
  II. A Building with Holiness (Hag. 2:8, 9; I Cor. 3:16 (Hearts)
  III. A Benediction of Hope (Hag. 2:18, 19; Eph. 3:20 (Head)

FAITH AND PRAYER (Hab. 1-3)
  I.   The Prophet Is Troubled (v. 1)
  II. The Prophet Is Taught (v. 2)
  III. The Prophet Is Triumphant (v. 3)

PRAYER FROM THE BELLY OF HELL (Jonah 1:17; 2:1, 10)
  I.   Jonah's Dilemma (v. 17)
  II. Jonah's Despair (vv. 1-6)
  III. Jonah's Devotion (vv. 7-9)
  IV. Jonah's Deliverance (v. 10)